Looking for a Lamb

©2005 Tony Woods

Marton Publishing LLC

Unless otherwise noted, Scripture quotations are from the Holy Bible, New International Version, Copyright 1973, 1978, 1984, 1998 by International Bible Society.

ISBN 0974984140

In Loving Memory

To Trevor, an all-American kid who started and finished his life in Japan, the country he loved. The Japanese tongue could never quite pronounce the "r"s and "v"s, and so they called him "Treasure". How prophetic a name, that with his passing Heaven has become a little more precious.

Foreword

This book is about as near a perfect combination of the personal, the touching, the exciting, and the humorous that I ever remembering reading.

It is a treatise on coping with sickness and a death and beyond. As you read it you will run the gamut of your emotions of sadness, admiration, excitement, grief, gratitude and joy.

This is a presentation for those who have lost something or someone precious – this is a book for all of us. It walks us through the stages of shock, adjustment, management of grief and development of faith.

Looking For a Lamb is a not-to-be-forgotten manual for use in prayer and warfare, struggle and triumph, standing and profiting from loss.

Here is outlined a journey confronted by "lesser lambs" until at last there is the discovery of the Lamb of Lambs! As I read this book I was blessed in every chapter.

I predict for every reader a memorable experience and profitable as well!

Jack Taylor, President and author
Dimensions Ministries

Contents

A Special Thanks...

To my wife Marsha, who walked up the mountain by my side, who helped me discern the real motives of each lamb that crossed our path, and who gave me strength when my own was failing. We've seen a few mountaintops since then, haven't we?

Introduction

Then God said, 'Take your son, your only son, Isaac, whom you love, and go to the region of Moriah. Sacrifice him there as a burnt offering on one of the mountains of which I will tell you."

Genesis 22:2

"Where are we going, Dad?"

My son moves with the impulsive energy of a young calf, his light-footed steps in stark contrast to my own heavy tread. Looking at the glow in his cheeks, I can neither believe nor accept what I've just been told: that his days have already been numbered.

"Up there," I point with my chin to the mountaintop, now hidden by dark clouds.

"Cool."

But it's not cool, I think to myself. It's more horrible than I can imagine: a father's worst nightmare. And yet the message that burned into my heart was unmistakable. Take your son to the mountaintop. There he will die.

I thought of Abraham, the man of God. The man who had waited for so long and who was finally blessed with a son they named Laughter: Isaac. The man whose faith was tested on a mountain in the region of Moriah. That son also questioned his father. He knew that they were going to the mountaintop to offer a sacrifice to God. But where was the sacrificial lamb? "God will provide a lamb," Abraham had answered, and I believe that with every fiber of his being, he hoped that it was true. God did provide, at the last possible moment, and father and son descended together. But that was then. What about today?

—

Indeed. What about today? Is this particular traveler and his son alone in their journey, or is it possible that others are also experiencing the gut-wrenching tragedy known as "the grief process"? It really *is* a process, you know, made so by countless repetitions by countless pilgrims. Grief can be triggered by something as casual as a headache, or as attention-demanding as the squeal of tires on wet pavement. Grief can come after the fact, such as in the loss of a loved one, or in anticipation, as we wait for something unwelcome. It can cloak itself in the searing pain of physical trauma just as easily as in the dawning realization that a relationship has lost its passion. Anytime our lives do not fit our expectations, we are susceptible to the crippling power of grief.

The first challenges to my own expectations came at an early age, just as I was beginning to think I had the world figured out. I remember the day clearly, as if it were yesterday. Mrs. Tibbits looked over the top of her glasses, opened the Sunday School quarterly and cleared her throat, a sign to our class of 10-year-old boys that it was time to begin.

"Class," she said, looking directly at me, I suppose because I was the one most in need of settling down, "today we're going to look at a boy in the Bible who was just about your age."

All right, I thought, somebody I can identify with.

"His name was Isaac, and one day God spoke to his father. He said, 'Abraham, I want you and Isaac to climb to the top of that mountain over there.'"

"Was there snow on it?" I asked eagerly. "Did they have to use ropes?"

"No. Anyway, God told Abraham to take Isaac to the top of the mountain, and offer him up as a sacrifice."

"What does that mean, Mrs. Tibbits?" Eugene asked. "What's a sacrifice?"

"That means, Eugene, that Abraham was supposed to kill Isaac and burn his body on an altar as a gift to God."

Wait a minute. This was no longer the kind of Bible story I'd been hearing at bedtime. It sounded more like the kind of movie that my Mom wouldn't let me go to. You can be sure that I paid great attention to the rest of the story that day.

I was shocked, and a little uneasy at the thought that God, who just last year I had professed to believe in, might turn out to be something less than the "Good Shepherd" Mrs. Tibbits had assured me He was. After all, I was a boy myself, and like she said, probably about Isaac's age at the time of the story. While my father was no Abraham, I could see that he took his faith seriously. What if God gave *him* that kind of command? In that case, *I* would be the other part of the story, a part I had no interest in playing.

3

But as my Sunday School class came to the end of the story of Abraham and Isaac that day, I was greatly relieved to see that God was only testing the man. It seemed that He never intended to carry it through; He just wanted to see if Abraham was willing to obey. At the time, of course, something in the back of my mind immediately sent up a red flag. I had been told that God was not bound by time, and while I couldn't quite catch what that meant, I did understand that God knew perfectly well what the future would hold. If that were the case, I thought, then why did He have to perform experiments on His people in the first place? If I had only had a little more Sunday School under my belt, I might have moved right then into the conclusion that it was *Abraham* and not God who needed the test. But for the moment, my relief over the fact that God was not a "mean man" put to an end any more worries.

Then I became a father. From that point on, every time I came across the familiar Genesis story, I saw it from a whole new point of view. Now it wasn't *me* who was the potential victim. If it was, then I would just have to work out in my mind how I would have escaped that situation. Now, as a father, I had to place myself into the role of Abraham, where I was not the victim (except that of God's dealings with me) but rather an antagonist, sent out to kill my own flesh and blood. The thought horrified me, and while I tried to tell myself that God would always remain first in my life, I was telling Him at the same time, "Please don't make me prove that!"

Of course, proof for any idea is almost always open to doubt, especially when the thing you're trying to prove (such as a willingness to kill or die) has to remain in theory. In Abraham's case, he didn't actually have to kill his son, but just come to the "point of no return" where nothing short of Divine intervention would have kept him from going through with it. *Willingness* to do something might pass as acceptable proof. On another level, willingness to *allow* something could also say to the world, "Hey, I'm really serious about this". It was at this level that my own journey up the mountain of faith found expression. Notice that I am not suggesting here that I "passed" some kind of Abrahamic test; only that I was subjected to one. I'm not sure I could ever demonstrate beyond a doubt any measure of faith, and even if I could, it would still need to be tested in the heat of any future circumstances. Just as life itself requires daily sustenance, the living of that life must be held up constantly before a standard of excellence in an effort to plumb the depths of faith.

For that reason, I believe that all of us, at any point in our lives, are on our way up some kind of mountain. It may be as well-marked and easily-negotiated as coming to grips with the kind of language we use among our friends, and deciding whether or not we glorify God with our lips. On the other hand, it may be the kind of mountain which shakes us to the very roots of our faith, bombarding us with doubts and fears concerning the existence of God Himself. Whatever the nature of the mountain, I say again: at this moment it is quite likely that you are in the midst of an ascent which will test the mettle of your faith. And like Abraham, you cannot help but ask, "How far do I have to go? Will God stay the knife at the last moment, or will I have to see this thing through to the very end?"

In the fall of 1991, a mountain loomed before me the likes of which I had only seen in my nightmares. For eight long months, I struggled up the forbidding slopes, desperate for an end to the ordeal. The end did come, and as I strain now to make out the path ahead, I don't see a valley stretching out to the horizon; but I do see a whole range of mountains which I have yet to cross. The very sight of it is enough to drive me to the point of despair. But I've been to that point before and discovered that strength for the moment was never lacking, and so I push ahead. In fact the journey does not seem as impossible as it certainly would have a few months ago, and the reason is that in the process of scaling the mountain that now lies behind me, I learned a few skills along the way. I also learned to recognize some of the pitfalls which will no doubt show up again. I want to share with you, fellow climber, some of the things I've seen, and if the opportunity presents itself, to learn what discoveries you've made along the course of your own journey.

I'd been a Baptist missionary to Japan since 1978, along with my wife Marsha and our two boys, Trevor and Nathan. Trevor was three years old when we first arrived, and Nathan was born in 1981. It was a fine line to walk, balanced between two cultures, but

I believe the boys handled the adjustments well. Coming up through the Japanese school system, they never had a problem speaking what a 17th century Jesuit missionary called "the devil's language." Unlike their parents, who struggled through two years of language school and still pray frequently that we won't mistakenly say something obscene, Trevor and Nathan both sloughed off the mysteries of Japanese and went outside to play with their friends. Through trial and error, positive and negative reinforcement, and language experimentation which only a child would dare to try, in a very short time both boys were considered "fluent," at least as far as the expectations of their ages. On more than one occasion, Marsha and I had to rely on their ability to communicate to get us out of situations involving telephone calls and strangers at the door who didn't happen to attend the same language school as we had.

With their blond hair and freckles, the boys never went anywhere without a crowd of observers. "Oh! Gaijin!" was one of the first expressions they heard. "Gaijin" means "foreigner" in Japanese, and we soon learned that this was to be our handle for as long as we lived in this country. With several generations of isolation behind them, the Japanese are still very much aware of their distinction from the rest of the world, and have gone to great lengths to protect that status. At first, the boys were a little put off by the constant attention, but with time learned to appreciate it, even going so far as to relish it. I still remember the first time we returned to the States for a visit when Trevor was six years old. Going into a department store, he went directly to the clerk, expecting to be made over and perhaps given a gift of some kind, as so often happens in Japan. When he was ignored instead, the shock was almost enough to drive him to tears. "That lady doesn't think I'm cute!" he said in a tone that sounded more like a threat. At that point, we began to realize what an impact life in Japan was having on our family, and readjusted our lifestyle to try and include a healthy, but not inappropriate self-image.

The years passed, and our boys thrived. Nathan developed an uncanny sensitivity toward animals, gaining the reputation of one who could make friends with any dog in town. Trevor, on the other hand, found mechanical things his forte. By the age of nine, he could disassemble any piece of machinery that had the misfortune of coming his way, and by the time he turned thirteen was learning how to put them back together again. He shared similar interests with his three best friends, Katsuya, Makoto and Jun. Together they made an unbeatable team, and spoke of the time when they would build their own business, living all over the world in unbridled luxury. During the course of growing up, the three Japanese boys came to know Jesus Christ as Trevor did, and the spiritual side of their maturing added an exciting dimension to the relationship. As members of the same church, they were always busy on various projects, from teaching English classes for other young people to putting together a Christian music band. Folks were a little taken aback at first when the boys performed the popular song, "Stand by Me" at church, but as they explained, the words express the kind of friendship which Christ Himself spoke of when He said, "Greater love has no man, but that he lay down his life for his friends." This was the kind of friendship Trevor had with Katsuya, Makoto and Jun; and it was the kind of friendship they preached was possible with Jesus Christ.

In 1990, we returned to the States for a one year home assignment, teaching at Golden Gate Baptist Seminary in San Francisco. By this time Trevor had reached the unbelievable age of fifteen, going on twenty, discovering everything from girls to cars in what seemed like the space of a few short weeks. He began to plunge into new depths spiritually, too, finding that the faith he had inherited from his parents was becoming uniquely his own. The year in California had been a growing time for all of us, but by the fall of 1991, we were all ready to get back home to Japan. We decided to make it an adventure, driving what was left of our old furlough car as far as Anchorage, Alaska, then selling it or giving it away and boarding the plane for Japan from there. By now, Trevor had a driver's license, and thought he had seen a bit of Heaven when I told him he could help drive. As it turned out, for the first week I was lucky to get a hand on the steering wheel at all; Trevor displayed a natural skill for handling a car, as we all had suspected he would, and so were more than willing to let him have the experience of taking us north.

Two days out of Anchorage, we broke camp and were loading up when Trevor said, "Is it okay if I don't drive today?"

That was the last thing I had expected to hear, and asked, "Why? What's the matter?"

"I just don't feel so good. My back is sore and my stomach feels upset."

All that day, he lay in the back of the car, quietly staring out at the beautiful Alaskan mountains. He didn't eat all day, and for a growing fifteen-year-old, this caused us some concern. Arriving in Anchorage, we took him to a local clinic, where preliminary tests indicated that he probably had picked up a kidney infection. "Nothing to worry about," we were told. "Just get lots of rest and take this medicine."

Two days later, Trevor was no better, and still hadn't eaten, so we took him back to the clinic. This time the doctor looked more concerned, and said, "It's possible he could have a case of mono. I'd better do a blood test." That night as we waited in our motel room, the phone rang. It was the doctor. "Mrs. Woods," he began when Marsha answered, "I need all of you down here right away. The tests are not too encouraging."

Driving down to the clinic, I told Trevor that we didn't know what was up, but it could be serious. "Well," he said, "if it's really serious, I want to say two things now: I'm not afraid to die, and I want to go back to Japan." I didn't know then how significant those words would become. Eight months later, almost to the day, he repeated them again after being told that he had only hours to live.

Arriving at the clinic, the doctor met us at the door, made us as comfortable as possible and began. "Of course you understand that these tests are inconclusive. But I can say with 99% certainty that your son has acute lymphoblastic leukemia. The words hit like a bucket of ice water. "But that's impossible!" I said. He's been perfectly healthy this whole trip. It only started four days ago when..."

"That's why they call it 'acute'," he said as gently as he could, then went on, "We don't have the proper treatment facilities here in Alaska, so I need to insist that you get on the next plane to the lower Forty Eight and put Trevor into a hospital there. I'll make the arrangements now if you'll just give me a state."

The next eight hours was like coming out of sedation. At times there would be a flurry of activity, as we called family, located a travel agent and proceeded to dump excess luggage. Then things would settle into a dull roar of semi-consciousness, when we'd retreat into ourselves and try to deny what was happening. At one point, I went outside, presumably to pray, but in fact to get away from a situation that was terrifying me. "How can You let this happen, Lord?" I cried. "We're on our way back to Japan, to the land You've called us to. People are waiting there. People who still need to know about You. Would You stand by and let something like this keep us away?"

All night I prayed for a miracle: that I would wake up and find it was just an incredibly realistic nightmare; the doctor would call apologetically and say that the blood sample had been switched by mistake.

"That's okay," I would say. "These things happen. Don't worry about it. We're on our way back to Japan."

But the nightmare refused to end and the doctor never called. By 7:00 the next morning, we were on a plane headed for San Francisco. I prayed again, only this time in a way that I had never prayed before. "Lord," I said, "if this is really what it looks like, then please, please *please* make this plane go down right now. End it all before we have to suffer another day of this."

Even as I prayed, I realized that I was making no allowance for the rest of the passengers on board, who might not have been quite so anxious to meet their Creator. But at the moment, I didn't care. All I cared about was the fact that cancer was staring us right in the face, and I couldn't bear to look at it any longer. I was willing to pay any price to make it go away; even if it meant taking what belonged to someone else in order to pay it.

San Francisco saw the fulfillment of our worst apprehensions. Yes, they said, it was leukemia. Furthermore, it was probably one of the more vicious varieties. "Of course there's always hope, but..."

Each day seemed to be determined to present us with even greater cause for despair than we had known the day before. One of the first reactions to the chemotherapy was diabetes. Daily injections of insulin were the rule, and for Trevor, who had always been paranoid about needles, this was hell on earth. He did learn to deal with it, though, and before long was actually giving himself the shots. Next the doctors discovered tumors along his backbone, which called for increased medication, accompanied with daily radiation treatments. That brought new meaning to the term "sick", and along with losing all his hair, contributed to making him a pretty miserable guy in the space of a few short days.

We moved to Colorado, in order to be close to family, and I thought, here at least we'll have the beautiful Rocky Mountains to take our minds off our misery. Trevor never had a chance to see them. The chemotherapy attacked his central nervous system, resulting first in excruciating pain which no amount of medicine could relieve, followed by loss of muscle control. In one day, he was transformed into a writhing mass of agony, bedridden and almost insane from the torment. Standing by his bedside in the dark hours of the night, I would rub his feet and say, "Hang in there, Trevor, God's right here with you."

"I *know* He's here," he would cry, "but what's He going to do?"

And I didn't have the slightest idea.

For eight months, the nightmare continued. Sometimes we would see a little relief, and dare to hope that things had turned the corner. Then a new wrinkle would hit like a boxer's uppercut, and we'd be left reeling in despair. Finally one morning in February, the doctor came and said, "I need to talk to Trevor alone. The medicine is not working, and I don't believe he can last more than a few hours. He's old enough to hear this, and I would rather he not be distracted by your presence."

Numb, we waited in the hall while she went in to talk to our baby. A few minutes later, she emerged, a look of surprise on her face. "I've never seen a more mature response from any patient. When I told him he was about to die, he just said, 'I'm not afraid to die; and whether I die or not, I want to go back to Japan.'"

Trevor hung on for two more days, facing each setback with courage, and even a sense of humor. When one of the nurses commented on the fact that he was outgrowing his pajamas, he said, "Yeah, they used to tell me how tall I was getting; now they tell me how *long* I am."

On Friday night, his kidneys failed, and he started slipping away from us. As we tried to watch a program on TV, he would keep drifting off, then apologize and promise to pay closer attention. By late evening, he was more asleep than awake, and for the first time in several months, I noticed that his legs were straight. Until now the pain had been so intense that he kept them bent almost double. The doctor came in again and said, "Frankly, I don't know why he's still with us. It almost seems as if he's waiting for something."

We remembered his desire, repeated almost daily for the last eight months, to get back to Japan and his friends. We shared that with the nurses on duty, and thanks to a great deal of cooperation were able to get a long distance phone call placed from his bedside. Thirty minutes later, Katsuya, Makoto and Jun were gathered at one house in Japan, and we called them. One by one, they spoke into the receiver as we held the phone to Trevor's ear. "Hang in there, Trevor!" they shouted in Japanese. "We'll see you soon!"

There was no indication from Trevor's expression that he heard or understood them, but immediately his heartbeat, which had been racing at 160 beats per minutes, slowed to thirty. Less than half an hour later, as we held him in our arms, his breathing slowed to a stop, and I prayed, "Lord, have we missed anything at all? Is there anything else I should have done, or is this the time for Trevor to come to you?"

In answer, Marsha and I were given a sense of peace, which lasted the rest of the night. We still had no idea why this whole ordeal had been necessary, but the outcome had never been in doubt. Returning home the next morning, Marsha took her journal, a spiral notebook she had begun in Alaska on the day he was diagnosed. "Today, the doctors told us Trevor has leukemia," the first words read. From that time, she had faithfully recorded events and impressions every day until now. Opening the journal to make the last entry, she was stunned to find that there was only one page left. She filled it with the words, "Today Trevor went to be with the Lord," and closing the book had to understand that God was not surprised by this ordeal, nor by its outcome. The words of Psalms 139:16 came to me, first as a taunt then gradually as a source of peace:

"...Your eyes saw my unformed body. All the days ordained for me were written in Your book before one of them came to be."

Even from the beginning, both Marsha and I had to understand and accept the fact that God knew perfectly well what was going on in our family. There were just too many indications to believe otherwise. Ours was never a case of doubting God's existence in the face of grief, but rather as C.S. Lewis so aptly put it in *A Grief Observed* a case of "coming to believe dreadful things about Him."

Time and again in moments of desperate soul searching, I was brought back to the story of Abraham and Isaac. Here was a man who obviously could not deny the reality of God's Hand on his life; but what must he have thought at the horror of such a touch? Surely he experienced some of the same emotions I was feeling. He had to have considered options to the appalling task he'd been given. The Bible is strangely silent concerning Abraham's emotions during this test of faith, and I suppose it's because God is the focus here and not the man. And yet, as the man in this particular ordeal, I have to consider my own emotions in light of Who I perceive God to be. How can I deal with what I'm feeling and still maintain faith in God? How did Abraham manage it?

All these questions were rolling around through the remnants of my broken heart shortly before Trevor died as I went to preach at a church pastored by an old friend and former fellow missionary. Ted Savage and his wife had been models for us when we were short term volunteers in Zambia in 1973. Their obvious faith was illustrated beautifully in their love for the people to whom God had sent them to minister. Now in the same fashion, they were serving a congregation in Colorado Springs, and I was looking forward to seeing them again and perhaps finding within myself some of the same Divine spark that was lighting up their lives. But as I came to the end of my message that Sunday morning, I found my strength beginning to leave. How could I stand up here and talk about how good God was, when I wasn't sure about it myself? How could I testify to God's faithfulness when I had yet to experience it in this time of grief and frustration?

Somehow, I got to the end of the message and stood at the front of the church while the invitation hymn was being sung. People came forward, but fortunately for all of us, there were other elders to receive them. I was spared the further challenge of trying to minister to those in need while my own poverty was so evident. Finally I fell to my knees there at the altar and cried. I tried to form some kind of prayer: anything that would speak to the torment in my soul. But nothing would come. My mind was completely overloaded with grief, so that the only thoughts I could comprehend were the questions which had so overshadowed everything else lately: Why, why, why?

Gradually, I was aware that Ted was beside me, his hand resting on my shoulder. I listened to see if in his prayer there was some word of encouragement that I could cling to, but was surprised to find that he had nothing to say either. He was crying, just like me. We wept together for awhile, then finally Ted spoke.

"Lord," he began, "we don't know why all this has come about, and we don't understand the half of it. We only know that we're hurting, and only You can bring relief. Oh God... oh God, we're looking for a lamb!"

There it was. The passage that had been so much a part of this process. Like Abraham, I too was being subjected to a loathsome task; not that I was being commanded to kill my son, but that I was being commanded to walk with him up the mountain of his death, knowing full well that God could make everything right with a single word: a word that refused to be spoken. And so I walked, and cried, and prayed; and all the while searched desperately for a lamb. Abraham was given one; wouldn't I be granted the same mercy? Would faith carry us to the top, and then reward us with healing? It had happened so often before, in our own lives as well as in the lives of those around us; surely, this time as well, God would provide a lamb of sacrifice, to be offered up in the place of my son. With every step, I had searched in desperation for that lamb I knew had to be there... Something, someone, some *miracle* was waiting right around the next bend. It was just up to me to find it and claim it for God's glory.

And there were lambs along the way. Each day brought new hope, new ideas that maybe this was the one: the way out we'd been looking for. My hands would reach out in joyful anticipation... then draw back in horror as I realized each time that this was not the lamb I had been seeking. There were lambs out there, all right, but they were not of the sacrificial variety. Some claimed to be, but were not. Some tried to be, but could not. And still I searched, until finally I came to the top of the mountain and discovered the truth which even Abraham could only dream about, but never knew in his own lifetime.

This book is an accounting of my search for a lamb, and of the discoveries I made in the process. Such accounts from other strugglers have been extremely helpful to me, and it is my prayer that this contribution will also find opportunity to be of comfort to someone else in grief. The revelations are not new, by any means: only stated from another perspective. But in the variety of perspectives we all have to offer, God has allowed us a wonderful opportunity to scan the dimensions of His love for us. Your own perspective, fellow climber, has value as well. Don't hesitate to share it with another. Together as we seek the pinnacle of our faith, may we look only to that Lamb of Lambs: the One Who is able and willing to be the sacrifice we so desperately seek.

Even as multifaceted as its expressions, grief does prefer certain predictable "stages" which can be identified. And in that fact is our hope: if we can see the beast for what he is, then we can prepare for him. We can overcome him. By God's grace, we can survive the "grief process" and emerge stronger than before. In the eight chapters to follow, we will see eight lambs, each representing a step along the road through grief. All but one is a deceiver. Examine each lamb carefully, and consider his offer. Have you met him before? You will almost certainly meet him again, for if there is anything certain about life's journey, it is this: grief is the dark contrast which gives joy its brilliance. We cannot avoid it, but then neither must we embrace it. Let us know it for what it is, accept it as a part of life, and use it as a tool for growth.

For Discussion:

1. How would you compare one person's grief brought on by physical pain to another's grief caused by the loss of a loved one? Can grief, in fact, be "graded"?

2. Would you agree that grief is inevitable in every life?

3. Respond to the statement (above), "We cannot avoid it [grief], but then neither must we embrace it."

For further study and background:

Read the story of Abraham and Isaac in Genesis 22:1–19. Consider:

1. Abraham was living in a time and place where child sacrifice was common.

2. God was in the process of setting Abraham apart, declaring to him that "I will make you very fruitful; I will make nations of you, and kings will come from you." (Gen. 17:6)

3. As Omniscient Creator, God knew Abraham perfectly. Testing his faith was not in order for God to learn something He did not know about the man, but for the man to learn something about himself and about his God.

Chapter One

The Lamb of Anger

*In your anger, do not sin. Do not let the sun go down
on your anger.*

Paul (Ephesians 4:26)

The mountain becomes steeper and we begin to
struggle. At first, it seems almost comical, to scramble
three steps up only to slide back two. We make jokes
about our clumsiness and it feels good to laugh. After
awhile, the laughter and the joking are put aside as
fatigue gives way to despair. Finally we stop to rest,
but one look at the gathering darkness causes me to
blurt out, "God help us if we have to spend the night
on this mountain."

A noise off to the left catches my attention. A
lamb, standing motionless, staring at me with an
expression which can only be contempt. For some
reason, I'm not surprised to hear him speak.

"God has no intention of helping you," the lamb
is saying to me through clenched teeth. "He just wants
to see you make a fool of yourself. He likes watching
you squirm. He likes seeing your son hurt. He thinks
you can't touch him, up there on his big throne. But
He's wrong. You *can* touch Him. Your anger can reach
all the way to the heavens. There is no part of the
universe which cannot feel the wrath of an angry
man."

Like his master, Satan, the lamb of anger is a liar, but he is also shrewd. He knows that I'll turn away in disbelief if his story is too far fetched. But just as I'm about to raise an eyebrow in doubt, he throws in enough truth to pull me back.

"You *can* touch Him," he'd said. I look in my heart, and know that much is true. God desires fellowship. I have the freedom to give or withhold fellowship, so I have the ability to affect a desire that God Himself feels. God wants my worship. By refusing to worship Him, I withhold something from Him which He cannot give Himself, at least not in the way He has created things. As an all-powerful God, He doesn't *need* me, but He *wants* me. Yes, I think, I *can* touch God; and right now I'm angry at Him. I might as well be honest.

As if the lamb had read my mind, he says, "That's right. Give honest expression to your anger. Don't hold it inside. Shout to God how you feel about him. Tell him what a sorry ruler He is. Do you want to hurt something? Go ahead. Hurt me."

For a moment my anger is averted by the lamb's offer. Hurt *him*? But the object of my anger is *God*, not him. What good would it do to attack something else? It seems the best I can hope for would be to stand before the heavens and shake my fist at God. But as I stand there, fist raised to the sky, I realize what a ridiculous sight that is. "Fists are not made for waving," I think to myself. "They're made for hitting." Swinging around, I see the lamb standing there, looking at me with an evil smile. Had he actually moved closer? I look back at my fist, still tightly clenched, then at the lamb, who at the moment is the embodiment of everything I hate: my frustration, my impotence, my fear. I swing. The lamb doesn't flinch, but stands still as I connect with his jaw. The blow sends him reeling backward two or three steps and for a moment his eyes roll back until I think maybe I've knocked him unconscious. But then he straightens up and looks me square in the face, a tiny drop of blood on his mouth. "That's right," he says. "You'll show Him. Do it again!"

I close my eyes as a primal scream rises up in my throat and draw back for another swing. But just as I'm about to unleash my anger a second time, a voice speaks inside my heart. "Don't," the voice says. "You're only hurting yourself."

I'm puzzled for a moment by the voice. I've heard it before, but I'd forgotten about it. The anger inside me had tried to drown out the voice, but still it came through. I stop, my right hand drawn back and frozen. The lamb senses my hesitation and steps closer. "You can't quit now," it says. "You're just beginning to accomplish something! He hates you, don't you see? He hates you and wants you to hate Him!"

That last statement is foolish enough to bring me to my senses and make me hesitate again. I'm vaguely aware of pain, coming from my hand. Bringing down the fist I had poised to strike with, I notice a gash across two knuckles. Blood is seeping into the palm of my hand, carrying with it a tiny strand of wool. I look back at the lamb of anger, who is now showing real indications of fear.

"What are you doing?" it shouts. "Don't stop! Don't stop!"

I look closer at the lamb's mouth, where the blood is now beginning to dry. Suddenly, I realize that the blood is mine, and not his. I had merely struck his teeth. He could not be hurt; I can see that now. The more I strike him, the more grievous my own wounds will become.

"Get away from me," I shout, loathing myself almost as much as I do the lamb that stands before me, shaking with excitement.

"No!" it shouts. "The anger within you is *good*! You can use it against *Him*! Think of your dying son!"

—

We may try to deny the fact, but most of us are prone to violence. As we grow older, a certain degree of control keeps us in check, but the pot is on simmer and the lid is loosely fixed. An unexpected jolt, or a sudden increase in heat will nearly always result in a boiling cauldron.

Perhaps it's a part of our built-in "survival system", responsible for the release of both adrenaline and the reserve which would ordinarily control our use of it. Any of us could fill a book with examples of angry outbursts, and the damage which resulted. Child and spouse abuse is rarely a premeditated thing; in most cases it follows a situation where anger pushes aside common sense and lashes out at the first thing it sees. Tragically, that "first thing" is often a loved one.

Fear is a close relative of anger, and in fact it may be the same emotion in a different disguise. When in the first grade I beat up the older boys who had been taunting me all the way home for three days in a row, I'm not sure if what I felt was anger or fear. Certainly if I had thought of the possible consequences of striking a fifth grader with a lunch box loaded with rocks in the company of his peers, I would have felt nothing but sheer terror. But at the time I actually drew back my weapon and heard the comforting "shhhook" as the rocks repositioned themselves, it was not fear I was feeling, but anger. I was *mad* at these guys who were humiliating me. I didn't care what might happen afterwards; I only knew that right then, the moment was mine. I was going to wreak vengeance, and I was going to enjoy it.

Of course, those sudden flare-ups of temper, while destructive enough, are not the most vicious forms of anger. Much more deadly is the "controlled burn", the seething crater of hatred and spite contained within the heart and fed daily with fresh accusations, either real or imagined. First degree murder, being premeditated, is always a more serious offense than crimes of passion, for in the first case there is evidence of a capacity to kill which goes beyond the heat of the moment. Any one of us, given the right set of circumstances, might lash out and in the process bring injury where none was intended. But for one caught in the deceptive snare set by the lamb of anger, those "flare-ups" of temper, coddled and fed, can be raised up to new levels of intensity until they become a formidable force of destruction, burning outward toward those around us as well as inward, until the heart has been gutted out and nothing remains but a blackened shell. In the same way, anger toward God is an emotion which must be handled with extreme caution. I believe the early men of God were aware of that fact as well. When the writer of Ecclesiastes wrote that there is a "time to hate," perhaps he was speaking not of things as they *should* be necessarily, but rather of things as they *are*. The apostle Paul spoke not of the possibility of anger, but of what to do in its presence. "In your anger do not sin," he said in Ephesians 4:26. "Do not let the sun go down while you are still angry, and do not give the devil a foothold."

I could accept those words, and even preach them to others. But the acceptance wears thin in the face of a suffering child. Regardless of what God may have intended for eternity, when my child was writhing in pain, I wanted healing, and I wanted it *immediately*. I knew God could do it; I had witnessed such miracles firsthand. Just a Word was all He needed.

But as the weeks turned into months, and the leukemia not only persisted but brought with it a new meaning to the word *torture*, I began to experience an emotion which until that time I had carefully guarded against: I became angry at God. "Why would you do such a thing?" I demanded. "Why would you show me your power to heal, and then refuse to use it for the sake of my son? Do you enjoy watching him suffer? Obviously you must, or you'd be doing something about it."

Even as I spoke those blasphemous words, I knew I didn't believe them myself. The things coming from my mouth were not the words of a rational man. In fact, I was *not* rational; I was on the verge of insanity, driven by anger and its close relative, fear. The lamb of anger had met me on the mountainside, and I had vented my aggressions on him.

I think of Moses, trying to lead a rebellious people across a wasteland with nothing more than a promise of better days to keep them going. "If only we had died when our brothers fell dead before the Lord," they complained. "Why did you bring the Lord's chosen people into the desert, that we and our livestock should die here? Why did you bring us up out of Egypt to this terrible place? It has no grain or figs, grapevines or pomegranates. And there is no water to drink!" (Num. 20:3 ff).

If I were in Moses' position, I would have been hard pressed to not take such criticism personally. I think I may have been entertaining a few fantasies concerning some of those more detestable neck pains! And then, oh the glory of it all! God comes to say He is about to do something for His people again!

"What would it be this time Lord? Are You going to have the earth swallow up a few more dissenters as an example? Or how about parting another body of water while I lift my staff over it;

that's always good. No? You're just going to give us water from a rock? Well, okay; that worked great last time. Remember? I struck the rock with my staff, the water gushed out, and I got a little respect for a change. Just show me the rock and I'll... what's that? I can't hit it like last time? What am I... what? *Speak* to it?"

And so it went. Moses, tested and tried until he was at the point of unraveling, was told to do something for which his anger had little chance for expression. If he could at least have *cursed* the rock... but no, in spite of the welling anger within him, Moses was directed by God to simply speak; speak to the rock and nothing more. As it turned out, this was simply too much for the man. "Listen you rebels," he told the watching children of Israel, and by now Moses was already in rebellion against God himself, "to prove God is with us, do we have to bring you water out of this rock?" And then he proceeded to strike the rock, not once, but twice. The water was produced, but in the process Moses, this man of faith and vision of whom it was said spoke "face to face with God, as to a friend," lost not only his temper but his place in the promised land beyond the Jordan River. For that act of rebellion, he was consigned to the wilderness for the rest of his life, coming no closer to the land of milk and honey than a hillside overlooking it, where he died.

If such a man as Moses could be so victimized by the lamb of anger, what chance do I have on the way up my mountain of grief? What chance do any of us have, faced with life's imponderables and death's uncertainties, of standing up to anger and defeating it?

On the mountain of my grief, I felt anger toward many people, including myself, and in the final analysis even toward God. I didn't understand why He chose not to heal my son. I still don't understand, but am sustained by the promise that someday, in eternity, I will. There will come a time, I'm told, when "I shall know fully, even as I am known" (I Corinthians. 13:12). But until that time of understanding comes, I also know this: anger at what I cannot comprehend serves no good purpose; and in fact this anger, if left unchecked will certainly destroy me. I've also come to realize that the lamb of anger is no acceptable sacrifice. He's a predator, and will not allow himself to be slain as a substitute for anyone.

For discussion:

1. Compare "crimes of passion" to "premeditated murder". Why are we more lenient in our judgment of the former?

2. Do you think anger and fear are close relatives? In what ways?

3. Is a person blinded by rage more likely to lash out at a stranger or a loved one? Why?

4. Should a person express his or her anger at God? Are there "proper ways" to do so?

5. Why did Paul stress the importance of resolving anger before "sundown" (Eph. 4:26)?

For further study and background:

Read the following biblical references to anger, then pray for wisdom:

1. Jesus: Matthew 5:21–22

2. God: Genesis 4:6–7; Psalms 30:4–5

3. Saul: I Samuel 20:30–31

4. David: Psalms 4:4

Chapter Two

The Lamb of Denial

Never Lord! This shall never happen to you!
Peter (Matthew 16:22)

It's dark as my son and I continue up the mountain. He stumbles, and I reach out to catch him. He's so light. I'm reminded of a time not so long ago when I would always carry him up a trail like this. He was too small then to negotiate the steps. Now he's big enough to walk on his own. But he's so light. I was told I wouldn't lose him until we reached the top, but that's not true. I've begun to lose him already.

"Where are you going?"

A voice in the darkness startles us both. We stop and peer along the side of the trail. There it is: a lamb, standing right next to the trail. I could reach out and...

"Where are you going?" the question is repeated.

"To the top of the mountain. With my son."

"Why?"

"Because I was told to. He said I had to go with my son, and... and..."

"And watch him die?" the lamb finishes the sentence I am unable to. I can't answer, so I simply nod and look away.

"Do you want to do this horrible thing?"

The question is absurd. "No! Of course not. I don't want to be here... I don't want to go there. I just want to go back to the way it was... if only, I mean, if I could just find..."

"A substitute?"

"Yes."

"I'm a lamb. Why look any farther?"

"Do you mean... you would be willing to..."

"I said so, didn't I? You don't have to be here in the first place, you know. I'm really amazed you've come this far, considering."

"But, don't we have to go to the top? I mean, a sacrifice must be made, at any rate."

"Why?"

"'Why?' Well, because *He* said so, and because I have to."

"You keep saying '*He* said so'; why do you always do what *He* says?"

"I thought..."

"Never mind. The fact is, you don't want to be here. You don't want to go there. You want a substitute. Here I am. Go home."

"But surely, I can't just, well, go home. Shouldn't I go on to the top with you?"

"Who says I'm going to the top?"

"But, you just agreed to be the substitute for my son. That means..."

"I know what it means, and I'm telling you for the last time, if you want me to take care of things, turn around and go home."

"But if you don't go then a sacrifice won't be made, and then He will..."

"There you go talking about *Him* again! Look, what did He say he would do if you refused?"

"Refused? Why, we never talked about that. I couldn't refuse *Him*."

Even in the darkness, I can see the half smile, half sneer. "That's the problem with your kind. You never consider alternatives. Think about it: He told you to do something, but never mentioned any options. How do you know there aren't any? And maybe better ones at that?"

"I don't know; I just can't imagine refusing *Him*."

"Can you imagine what's going to happen when you get to the top? Let me help. You're going to get there, and your son is going to be laid out on a stone table. He's going to be screaming in pain. He'll look to you for help, but by that time, you'll be powerless to stop it. He's going to *die* up there; and here you are, just the two of you, walking up there as if you were going to a picnic. Let me ask you this: what's the worst that could happen if you refused? You never considered it, did you? I'll tell you one last time, turn around and go back home. Forget this whole thing. It won't be nearly as tough as you think."

—

For most living things threatened with imminent danger, the fight or flight syndrome follows a fairly predictable pattern. Before resorting to teeth and claws, we usually find that a shot of adrenaline offers a pretty good chance for escape from most any attack. Since the bottom line is survival, most of us would opt for escape before confrontation any day.

I can imagine the same was no less true for Abraham, as he moved slowly to make preparations for the reprehensible task he'd been given. What was going through his mind as he loaded provisions and put his household in order? We can only speculate, but since the Bible doesn't seem to indicate that Abraham was too much different from any other man of his day, I think it would be safe to say that he must have at least considered alternatives to what God had commanded.

During my own journey up the mountain of grief, I too considered alternatives. The flight instinct was running overtime, telling me to get as far away from the situation as I could. In the early days of the ordeal, I had a particular aversion to being in the same room with my son. Normally, I'm a very positive type individual, even to the point of irritating those who consider themselves "realists." It doesn't matter how ugly the mess may be; I can usually find something in it to admire. But with Trevor, it was different. Seeing him sick was like a knife in my own heart. Try as I might, I just couldn't keep the smile pasted on my face. So I stayed away as much as I could.

When the diagnosis first came, I almost ran outside. I mumbled something to Marsha about needing to be alone to pray, but the truth was, the reality of the situation so terrified me that I couldn't remain. I don't remember getting on the elevator, but somehow I made my way to the ground floor and found myself in the hospital parking lot. What struck me was the sight of so many people leaving. Men, women, families, doctors, nurses: they were getting in cars and driving away. They could do that, and I envied them so much I couldn't take my eyes off each car as it pulled away, shifted gears and disappeared into the night.

"You could do that, you know."

The voice was faint, but I got the message. It was true. There was nothing holding me there in that parking lot except some spoken promises and a vague idea we call commitment. No one would arrest me if I just got in my car, started it up, and drove away. I could be in British Columbia by this time next week. I've always wanted to go there. I could probably get a job doing just about anything...

What was I talking about? This was ridiculous! I wasn't about to leave. I *loved* my family, and I had no intention of deserting them now when they needed me more than ever. I turned to go back into the hospital, and was horrified to find that I was holding the car keys in my hand. Had I really seriously considered running? I sloughed it off as shock and went back to my family. The days turned to weeks. The prognosis became more grim with each test. Fatigue was wearing us all thin. It had been, I don't know, *months* since any of us had slept all night without an interruption. I wondered if all those stories about Chinese torture were true; the ones about sleep deprivation. One of these mornings, I might just crack up. I mean, just look in the mirror, and see a crazy man staring back at me. I never for a minute believed I'd be capable of doing what some of those guys in the newspaper were reported to have done. Give them a rifle and an ax to grind and people died. They were crazy. But now, I could see where *I* might become crazy. How much of this can a person take before something snaps and he becomes someone else? We only had to observe other parents at the hospital to realize there were many ways to deal with grief, some acceptable, some not.

It was about then that I began to realize that the lamb of denial was still there with me. He hadn't gone away that night on the hospital parking lot as I thought he had. He'd simply slipped around behind me and changed his approach. I no longer entertained ideas of making a mad dash for the car and heading off for the gold fields. I never had seriously considered it anyway, but the fact that the options had come into my mind prepared me for the more believable suggestions.

"Of course you wouldn't just run away," the voice behind me said. "That would be stupid. And you're not stupid. If you left, you'd do it right. You'd have money in the bank and a hat full of ideas. Such as..."

Then my mind would drift through fields of "what ifs": what if it came to that; what if I really *needed* to leave; what if there was no other way? I'd be smart to have a plan in mind. And so the thoughts would come and go, and all the while I would be telling myself, this is never going to happen. I'm just exercising my mind. Just thinking of scenarios, just in case.

Once in a while, I'd be hit with a hard fact which supported my "what-iffing". Eight out of ten couples who lose a child are in some stage of separation or divorce within a year. That's not speculation; that's truth. I could see how something like that could happen. When grief sweeps over you so completely, it takes every bit of perseverance you can muster just to keep your sanity and survive from one day to the next. Married couples are usually able to lift each other up during difficult times, but when both are sinking, there is neither energy nor motivation to reach out and help each other very much. A strong marriage can survive times like this for awhile, but eventually the edges begin to fray. At one point, Marsha and I made a promise to each other. We agreed not to take anything the other said personally for at least a year, but just chalk it up to grief. That helped, and I strongly recommend it to other couples in stress.

But before we came to that decision; in fact before Trevor died, the temptation to deny the situation by escaping from it became more and more insidious, the suggestions more subtle.

"It wouldn't have to be permanent," I heard myself being told. "People separate all the time, then get back together. Look in the mirror: you're *dying* from stress. Avoid the pain of the moment and you'll survive in the long run. Your family will forgive you in time. You'll all look back on these days and say, 'it was worth it'."

Less basic than physical flight but just as much a part of denial is the temptation to deny the reality of the moment. That is, to see the situation as something besides what it appears to be. Abraham would have been a rare individual indeed if he had not tried to read something else into God's command. After all, in those days, the worship of Baal was evident everywhere. God's people were a definite minority in that land where first born children were routinely sacrificed for the sake of the rest of the family. As Abraham watched his neighbors endure such grief willingly out of a belief in their god, he must have thought: could I do that? Do I love my God any less, that I would not also be willing to make such a sacrifice? If such thoughts had been a part of his consciousness, then it would have come as no big surprise to hear the dreaded words for himself: "Yes. I want you to do the same thing."

But then he would have to search deep within his soul for the source of those words. Was it really God, or was it his own confused mind speaking? Abraham, after all, was not known for his clear perception of God's messages. When God told him he was to have a son in his old age, he waited expectantly for his wife Sarah to start knitting booties. But when several years had passed, he must have thought he'd missed something in the translation. Sarah too began to lose hope, and finally offered her handmaiden to

Abraham as the mother of the promised child. A child was born to the handmaiden, but eventually a child was also born to Sarah: the fulfillment of the promise. Looking back over that kind of experience, Abraham had to have felt at least a small degree of doubt as to his ability to understand exactly what it was God wanted him to do. And especially now, in the face of such an appalling command, the temptation to deny its reality must have been awesome. Is it so difficult to imagine him thinking, "Lord, I mistook Your Word once before... maybe I'm wrong about this, too."?

In the same way, I battled daily with my own perceptions of God's will for Trevor. It was reprehensible to think that God actually *desired* this kind of pain for us. Scripture seemed to be filled with assurance that this was nothing other than an enemy I had every right to confront.

"The thief comes only to steal and kill and destroy; I have come that they might have life, and have it to the full."
(John 10:10)

"He himself bore our sins in his body on the tree, so that we might die to sins and live for righteousness; by his wounds you have been healed."
(I Pet. 2:24)

"And I will do whatever you ask in my name, so that the Son may bring glory to the Father. You may ask me for anything in my name, and I will do it."
(John 14:13–14)

Looking at these and other scriptures, listening to the affirmations of friends whose walk with the Lord was evident, and feeling the assurance in my own heart, I was convinced: Trevor would not die of leukemia. God did not want it, God's people were praying against it, God's word is trustworthy. So for a time, our whole family enjoyed fresh hope, greeting each day with praise and worship in spite of the gloom and doom presented by the doctors and nurses who without hope understood only what they could see.

In a sense, we even took heart when things *did* appear worse: God was going to let things get about as bad as they could get before He stepped in, just so there would be no doubt as to Who was at work. A miracle is much easier to accept if the odds are unmistakably against it. "Heaven forbid that Trevor's healing be explained away as a tribute to medical technique," we comforted each other.

As Trevor's condition grew worse, we laughed at the reports and said to each other, "Well, he's just *tired*, you know." The doctors tried to understand our strange sense of humor, but for one who had never experienced God's miraculous power, it was difficult to comprehend. I realized something one night as I was talking with the nurse on duty, sharing with her my conviction that everything was going to be all right. Going about her work in the room, she turned away from me as she said, "Well, it looks to me like you're certainly in denial."

Faith in a sense *is* denial, I tried to explain. The Enemy is a deceiver, and would have us believe that the situation is hopeless. But by faith, we refuse to listen to his lies. We deny what appears to be real. We hold on to the Truth which we've received from God.

There is evidence that such denial is therapeutic, even apart from Christian circles. In a well-known test a few years ago, several people were selected who had warts. Half the group was told to do nothing for them, the other half was told to spend a preset period of time each day imagining the warts disappearing. Of course, most of the people in the latter group *did* lose their warts, so the tests became more specific. Now they were told to imagine only the warts on one hand, or on one side of the body to go away. Once again, the majority of those participating were amazed to discover that things happened pretty much as they imagined, and it wasn't long after that when the term "visualizing" became a popular term, especially among those identifying with New Age philosophies.

But such an approach to disease can only carry one so far. The body has demonstrated an incredible ability to heal itself, lending new meaning to Jesus' statement that the "Kingdom of God is within us" (Luke 17:21); but there are certain realities against which no man has yet been able to produce an effective antidote. Someone commented on the abundance of crutches and canes left at a popular shrine noted for the unusually high incidence of miraculous healings taking place there, but went on to observe that there was a distinctive lack of artificial limbs. Apparently even the miraculous has limits, at least this side of Heaven.

With the ability of hindsight, we can see now that in Trevor's case, leukemia was a reality which denial would not dislodge. There are those who would tell us that the problem was in the quality of our denial. If only we'd had more faith, we could have won out over the demon. Perhaps that's true. Maybe there will come a day when we discover a new "key" to faith, unlocking doors we can't even begin to imagine. But I must go back to that night in the hospital when Trevor drew his last breath. Holding him in my arms, I prayed with all the conviction I could draw forth. "Have I missed anything, Lord?" I asked. "If we *are* Your sheep, and know Your voice, would You let us lose our son out of ignorance?"

The peace that I felt then was an answer that I can accept for now. I still believe that God desires to heal us. I will never entertain the notion that He takes any pleasure in our sufferings; He's not that kind of God. And yet I accept the fact that certain realities persist, in spite of God's ultimate will for our lives. Jesus tried to prepare His disciples for those realities. "I tell you the truth," He said, "you will weep and mourn while the world rejoices. You will grieve, but your grief will turn to joy. A woman giving birth to a child has pain because her time has come; but when her baby is born she forgets the anguish because of her joy that a child is born into the world. So with you: Now is your time of grief, but I will see you again and you will rejoice, and no one will take away your joy" (John 15:20–22).

The process of death has often been compared to the birth experience. Here, on this side of Heaven, we're comfortable considering the circumstances, and have no real desire to leave this place. In the same way, an unborn baby, surrounded by the warmth and security of the womb, would be (and in fact is) terrified at the prospect of being ripped away, its lifeline severed and discarded. For those of us in the delivery room, the event is pure joy, but for the baby it is anything *but*. I can imagine the angels in Heaven witnessing my arrival in the Kingdom. I scream and cry out "No! Save me! Heal me!" while those on the other side are saying, "Glory! Another soul free from pain and the torment of the enemy. At last he can know the joy of his status as a Kingdom child!"

I witnessed my son's entry into the Kingdom, but not from the perspective of the other side. I had to observe it as one still trapped in a world of pain and dark terrors. And true to my nature, I had to cry out, "No Lord! Save him! Heal him!"

The Lord heard my cry, and He granted my request. But the reality of the moment was a knife in my heart which I could no longer deny. The joy of Trevor's going was diminished by the grief of his going. I miss him. I want him back. That's my reality today. But God is speaking to my broken heart, and saying, "There is a greater reality which you have yet to experience. Be patient, my child. Your time of knowing will come soon enough."

—

"I'll tell you one last time," the lamb repeats, "turn around and go back home. Forget this whole thing. It won't be nearly as tough as you think."

For the first time, my son speaks up. "I'm not afraid, Father," he says to me, all the while looking at the lamb. "If you're thinking of me, then don't. I know who owns me, and I know He waits for me. I'm not afraid."

Then I realize that *I* am afraid, and not simply for my son. There are worse things than dying, and the top of the mountain promises to offer them to me there. But if death is not to be my road today, then where is my fear, except in life itself? If I must live with this, then would I be better off to live it up there, with Him, or down in the valley, alone?

"Get away from me!" I shout to the lamb. "You have no interest in me, but only in hurting *Him!* I will *not* deny what He has given me, and I will not allow you to blind my sense with vain promises. You will not..."

I suddenly realize that the lamb is gone, and I'm only speaking to the darkness. Was he ever really there? A clap of thunder from high above us reminds me that *He* never left, and is still waiting at the top of the mountain. "Thank you," I say to my son. "You've made the way a little easier."

He smiles, and we set off again up the trail we have no desire to travel, but which we have no intention of leaving. A flash of lightening illuminates the way.

For discussion:

1. Have you ever experienced healing by sheer force of will? That is, have you concentrated your thoughts and prayers toward an affliction until it was overcome?

2. Is there room for denial in a life of faith?

3. Does the recognition of reality challenge your faith? How?

For further study and background:

Look up the following Scripture references to "denial":

1. Leviticus 16:31
2. Isaiah 5:23
3. Luke 9:23
4. James 3:14

How are these different from the kind of denial which grief produces?

Chapter Three

The Warrior Lamb

My first image of the Warrior Lamb is in silhouette, against the backdrop of the darkening sky. A golden ray of light from the setting sun illuminates a pair of magnificent horns, which gives his face the regal look of one who has never known defeat. By now, I have been defeated twice: once by Anger and once by Denial; and while those lambs have failed to halt my forward progress toward the summit, I have no illusions about my weakness. Seeing that the trail will pass just below where the Warrior is standing, I'm sorely tempted to seek another route which would avoid any contact with him. But there is no other way. I wait until my son is close beside me, then we move ahead together, hoping he won't speak. I'm disappointed.

"You will not escape your enemy by trying to avoid him, you know."

"What 'enemy' are you talking about?" I ask, trying to hide the fear that must be as evident to him as it is to me.

"You know perfectly well what enemy. It's the one who waits at the top of the mountain: the one who wants to steal your son." The lamb had been looking off in the distance when he first started speaking, but now he looks down, directly at me, finishing my unspoken thought. "To kill him."

I'm not sure whether to be relieved that this

beast has not identified himself as my enemy, or angry that he would display such a rebellious attitude toward the One who called me on this journey, "Wait just a minute," I opt for the latter. "How do you dare to call the One who made you your enemy?"

The lamb gave a snort of disgust and looked around him. "Just because I make something doesn't mean I'm its friend. Haven't you ever made clay figures for the sole purpose of destroying them in your war games? *He* has no love for you. If he did, then why are you on such a ridiculous mission? No, he thinks of himself as a conqueror, an almighty god! And once in a while he has to prove it by subjecting pawns like yourself to his cruel games. Mark my words, once he's finished his sport with your son, you'll find yourself back on your own, licking your wounds and wondering when you'll be required again."

Such words are unthinkable, and every part of my being rebels against hearing them. And yet... a part of me wants desperately to believe that the lamb speaks the truth. If he does, then perhaps my own rebellious thoughts are justified.

"Then what would you have me do?" I ask with as much acid as I can generate. "I suppose you'd like to see me storm the citadel and take down the tyrant. Or perhaps you'd like to do that yourself? You seem like a strong enough beast. Where's your army?

"Do you think that I stand alone, *human*? Is it only you who cannot see nature's rebellion all around? There is no corner of the universe where creatures like myself have dared to rise up and say 'Enough! We will bow down to your injustice no more.' No, I am not alone, but you soon will be. Go back to your home and count the *faithful*. I dare say you will find that you are a pitiful minority indeed.

I try to counter his verbal attack, but I cannot. He speaks just enough truth to prevent me from turning away. I *am* a part of a minority; I know that. The Master said so Himself. "Small is the gate and narrow the road that leads to life, and only a few find it" (Matthew 7:14). I only need to open my eyes to realize that most of the world I know is either complacent to the Master or else openly defiant. But does that mean that the outcome of this rebellion is in question? I voice my confusion, which the Warrior Lamb takes as acquiescence to his side. "But no one, man nor beast, could go against Him and hope to win."

"Exactly!" he cries, and with a ground shaking leap lands at my feet on the trail. "That's the mistake everyone makes. The fools thought they could march right into his throne room and toss him out. I could have told them that such tactics are doomed to failure. Why do you think he summons you to the mountaintop, and not some low-lying valley?" he asks, then answers his own question. "Because he must keep the high ground, that's why! By insisting that you come to him, he maintains the advantage. By the time you get there, you'll be too tired to fight, and the summit will offer no room for maneuvering. His victory is assured."

"So what do you suggest?" I can't believe I'm

allowing this conversation to continue. It's ludicrous, and yet somehow stimulating.

The lamb looks all around, then lowers his voice to a whisper. "You make *him* come to *you*. Let him see what it's like on a real battlefield, with more than one opponent to deal with." One more glance all around, and the lamb lowers his voice yet again. "Draw him down to us, and we will stand behind you; go to where he waits, and you go *alone*."

—

Man has always been a fighter; that much is obvious. Boys and girls may have different styles of fighting, but all are born for battle. The theologian Thomas Aquinas, when remarking about original sin, made the assertion that "If the newborn baby could, it would grab its mother by the throat and *demand* its milk," such is our predilection for selfishness and greed. It may be difficult for me to accept that image of a precious newborn, but it's not so hard to see when the child leaves the crib and advances into the playground. Supremacy is the goal and violence is often the means. It's the rare child who will not naturally fight for advantage, and of course that's the child who attracts the attention of parents and carers. "She's so docile. What's wrong with her?"

This is not to say that one must never fight. Our world would quickly destroy the pacifist, and whether we are fighting gravity in our attempts to learn to walk or whether we are fighting the Hitlers who would burn our homes, we must take up our positions daily and test our mettle. The Bible is a "war book" itself, encouraging believers to "Put on the full armor of God…" in our battle "against the rulers, against the authorities, against the powers of this dark world" (Ephesians 5:11ff). C. S. Lewis in his classic, *Mere Christianity*, made the claim that "Christianity is a fighting religion… in a world gone wrong," and furthermore that "God insists, and insists very loudly, on putting them right again" (pp37–38).

Perhaps there are those who struggle with the idea of fighting against men, but virtually no one will step back from the fight against disease. It's an enemy which deserves nothing less than total defeat, and we feel justified in using every weapon of mass destruction we hold in our arsenals. That fact was no less true than in my fight to save my son. The question was never, "Should I attack these tumors?" but rather, "What's the strongest medicine available? Teach me how to use it."

And use it we did, with the result that the cancer fairly quickly went into remission. We rejoiced, and thanked God for the tools He had given us: weapons against the curse for which we held no hesitation to employ against the faceless enemy called leukemia. It was a silly thing I know, but early on I even determined never to capitalize the word for the disease which struck my child. Perhaps the dictionary would demand such, calling it a "proper noun", but in my eyes there was nothing proper about it. It was evil, it was ugly, and I wanted it dead. End of story.

But unfortunately the story was not ended. A doctor who had been a veteran of many such battles warned me, "Don't be too quick to claim the victory. It's only in remission. You've managed to kill the weakest strains of the disease, but the survivors are still there, and multiplying. They'll be back, and the next time they won't be so easy to defeat."

He was right. In a few short weeks, Trevor's blood tests came back with the stomach turning news: the leukemia cells were back with a vengeance. Bigger guns were called for, and brought to bear. Radiation treatments went straight to the outbreak, killing the deformed cells, and tragically, many of the healthy ones. His hair fell out. He suffered nausea. He could no longer walk. But the doctor said that "desperate times call for desperate measures." The treatment, he explained, was horrific by intention. "Our mission," he said, "is to come as close to killing Trevor as we can, because that's the only way to kill the cancer that permeates his body."

Such words were like a knife in my heart, and many were the times when I would have to leave my son's room in order to cry. But along with the torment came another emotion which I had only read about in war stories. I had heard that many times on the battlefield when all seemed lost, there would be one or two who would rise up out of their own personal hell and accomplish the heroic. Afterwards, if they lived to talk about it, they would report a kind of "invisible line" (the novelist James Jones described it as "thin" and "red"), which they felt compelled to cross over.

Having done so, they no longer experienced pain, emotion, fear or mercy. They simply lashed out at anything and everything that stood in their way, often changing the course of battle.

Before leukemia invaded our family, my personal lines were fairly simple and predictable. They were marked by love for my children, a sense of decency and a love of God. In the day to day living of our lives, these lines were never challenged and rarely questioned. But with a horror such as that which was inflicted upon my son, all lines were down. I hated the treatments he had to endure, but I hated the disease more. I encouraged him every day to fight with every ounce of strength he had, and then demanded more. When the doctor said he must exercise to maintain muscle control, I drove him mercilessly. When he hesitated before any new procedure, I would remind him that he was tougher than anything they could throw at him. I referred often to the "man of steel" image I'd been given of him during his first spinal tap ("The Lamb of Anger"), and pressed him to endure and even to laugh in the face of his pain. This was war, I said, and we will prevail.

There's a scene from the movie, "The Never Ending Story", which Trevor and I watched together from his hospital room, and which bound us even more inseparably to our mission. Atreyu, boy hero from the mythical land of Fantasia, is trying to save the land from an encroaching force known as "The Nothing". But first he must battle the Morgue, a wolf-like creature. Just before the final conflict, Atreyu warns his enemy, "I will not die easily, for I am a warrior."

Hearing that declaration, I turned to look at my son, who had already stolen a glance in my direction. "That's you, you know," I said softly, and he nodded in reply. For both of us, this battle was the stuff of manhood, and we would show the world what we were made of. Bring it on, we said.

But those who have experienced a real battlefield will tell us that it's not always that clean cut, and never that heroic. In the midst of the horror, there is no swelling background music to spur the conqueror on. There is no shift to a minor key to warn us of impending danger. There is no delicate fade away of the camera, in order to protect our senses from that which is too horrible to behold. Real battle is a nightmare of sights and sounds, pain and terror, insanity and madness. The lines are indistinguishable at times, unstable at best. And it is here that the warrior faces his most treacherous foe: himself.

As Trevor's condition worsened and the doctors began telling us to prepare for the end, I crossed the line. I refused to believe what I was hearing. This was simply not acceptable. I fought harder, and when the enemy was not to be found, I set my sights on things which I *could* see. Trevor's brother, Nathan, my wife, my friends, the kitchen wall, and at the peak of my madness I set my sights on God.

I can recall exactly when that happened. I was driving back into the hospital after receiving a call from the doctor that "things were not going well." I could barely see to drive, so blinded was I by tears. I prayed out loud, and my prayers were no longer prayers of supplication; I was demanding.

"You can't do this, God!" I screamed. "It's not fair! It's not right! No! No! No! No!" Each exclamation was accompanied by a blow to the steering wheel of the car. I didn't care who saw me, as long as *HE* saw, and responded. As my energy began to drain and I found it more and more difficult to drive, I finally pulled off to the side of the road. An image had come into my mind, and I'm certain now that it was given to me by God. I remembered a time when I was very young, perhaps five years old. I had wanted something, I can't remember now what it was. But my father had refused, and I went ballistic. I cried, and when that didn't work I screamed. I fell on the floor and kicked anything within reach. My father bent down and picked me up, holding me close to his massive chest. I remember beating on his chest and screaming the same words I had just repeated: "No! No! No! No!"

As I was shouting those words, my emotions had lost all semblance of control. I was angry, I was frustrated, and I was determined to make someone pay. And at the moment, that someone was my father. I can't remember exactly how my father handled the situation that day, but I do know the lesson that he built into me: it's okay to be angry and frustrated. It's okay to tell your father how you feel. But it is *never* okay to strike him. He is the ultimate authority and he will be obeyed.

It should be clear to all that God has given us families in order to teach us about our relationship with Him. The Bible is filled with such images, from God as our Father (Romans 8:15), to we the Church as His bride (2 Corinthians 11:2), to every fellow believer as a brother or sister (Matthew 12:50). Pity the child who has missed this most precious of gifts, for it is through understanding of our role in the human family that we can better understand our role to God.

God is our Father, and as such we look to Him for our necessities, our well being and our instruction. Just as my human father taught me, so God teaches me that He is to be obeyed in all things, even when I don't feel like obeying. There are times, I must accept, when I simply do not know what is best, and it is then when I need my heavenly Father's instruction all the more. If I refuse that instruction, then I slip into disobedience, which leads to a road more horrible than I can imagine.

The Warrior Lamb met me at my weakest moment and offered me hope. "Your Enemy is up there, and he is outnumbered," I was told. "He holds the high ground, but you must draw him down." While the very idea of going into battle against God was reprehensible, I still listened to the Warrior, because he spoke from experience. He was right, after all, about God being outnumbered. Even a cursory glance around the world will show that His supporters are a small minority indeed. Even a so called "Christian nation" like America is trying to redefine itself apart from its spiritual roots. Bibles are removed from

schools, crosses and other Christian symbols are not
allowed on government property, and there is even a
concentrated effort in the nation's courts to have the
words, "Under God" removed from the pledge of
allegiance. The forces of rebellion are becoming more
emboldened each day, and the Bible tells me that it
will all culminate in one huge battle on the fields of
Armageddon. The rebels believe they have a fighting
chance for two reasons: first, because they are
numerically superior. I've always scoffed at that
reasoning, because as any believer knows, one plus
God is a majority. Anyone foolish enough to think that
the Creator of heaven and earth can be defeated by
sheer force of numbers must deserve what awaits.

But another thought has been suggested: it's
true that God is not impressed by the numbers alone,
but is it possible that He can be moved by the sight of
the souls for whom those numbers represent? If Satan
can say to God, "Defeat me if you will, but you will
have to destroy those you love in the process," would
that have any bearing on the outcome? Would God,
for the sake of preserving those whom he fashioned
and sent His own Son to die for, be willing to
negotiate? Satan apparently thinks so, and as a result
has done everything in his limited power to gather
around him men and women who have turned to the
Warrior Lamb. These are the rebels who intend to
carry the battle for the kingdom down to earth.

The battle began in the heavens, we are told in
the twelfth chapter of Revelation. There, Lucifer and
his followers attempted to overthrow the throne and

were cast out of heaven as a result. The battle continues in the earthly kingdom, and will continue until he and all who rebel against God will be cast away, once and for all. The Warrior Lamb knows from experience that a frontal attack within God's own kingdom is doomed to fail, but now he tries a different tact. "Draw him down from the summit," he tempts the pilgrim. "Bring him onto *our* domain, and He will find a much different situation."

And so it happened. "Who, being in very nature God, did not consider equality with God something to be grasped, but made himself nothing, taking the very nature of a servant, being made in human likeness. And being found in appearance as a man, he humbled himself and became obedient to death – even death on a cross!" (Philippians 2:6–8)

God left the high ground and came directly into the enemy's lair, leaving behind all pretensions of Divinity and power. Mano a mano. The rebels saw their chance and struck. The Son lay dead, and the world went dark. Three days later, the tables were turned and death itself was given a fatal blow (1 Corinthians 15:25), or so the Scriptures declare. But the Warrior Lamb has not given up so easily. Still he continues to fight, and to draw others onto his side. His cause is lost, and whether he knows it or not, his fate is sealed. But either out of desperation or out of rage, he intends to take as many of God's precious children with him as he can. "Come and join the fight," he calls. "We can win! We can set up our own kingdom, removed from his interference."

I remember a powerful scene from the play by Dorothy Sayers called "Man Born to be King". Baruch the Zealot has learned of Jesus and his plans to enter Jerusalem the next day. Here is an opportunity to strike a blow against the Roman occupation, he thinks. Dictating a letter to Jesus, he writes, "Baruch the Zealot, to Jesus of Nazareth, the Son of David, King of Israel: greetings. I have observed you, and I know who you are. To every man opportunity comes once and not again. The Priests and Pharisees are in league to deliver you to Rome; but the people are on your side, and I have men and arms. Give me a sign, for now is the moment to strike and seize your kingdom.

"When a king comes in peace, he rides upon an ass; but when he goes to war, upon a horse. In the stable of Zimri, at the going-up into the City, is a war horse saddled and ready. Set yourself upon him, and you shall ride into Jerusalem with a thousand spears behind you. But if you refuse, then take the ass's colt that is tied at the vineyard door, and Baruch will bide his time till a bolder Messiah come.

"Say only, *The Master has need of him,* and the beast is at your service."

See also Luke 19:29–31.

—

The Warrior Lamb repeats his promise: "Draw him down to us, and we will stand behind you; go to where he waits, and you go *alone.*"

I hesitate. His words are ridiculous, but no more than my own troubled thoughts. Here at least is an offer of hope. A glance toward the summit reminds me that only death waits for me there. Perhaps...

"You're wrong, and you know it."

I turn in shock to see my son standing just behind me. He's moved closer, and has reached out to lay one hand on my shoulder. "He's not going alone," he repeats, and I realize that he's speaking to the lamb. "I go with him, and together we go with the prayers of many. You have nothing to offer."

He squeezes my shoulder, and it prompts me to action. Without another word, we move past the Warrior Lamb, even as he protests our stupidity. We keep climbing, never looking back until we can no longer hear his voice. Finally, we stop to rest.

"That was a very brave thing you did, Son," I say. "Are you sure about this?"

"More than ever," he answers with a strength I didn't know he had. It's a strength I had almost lost, but as we moved on together, I felt it returning.

For discussion:

1. Why do you think Satan would continue to fight if he knows he has lost?

2. Is there a spiritual "high ground" from which the Christian can fare better in times of war?

3. Do you think that believers are really in the minority? Does that affect how you live?

4. How can one be a warrior while maintaining an attitude of humility?

5. Describe where you might see yourself in the army of God. Are you a foot soldier, an artillery officer, a pilot, a cook? Is one role more important than another?

For further study and background:

See what the Bible has to say about Satan and the rebellion he led. Some places to start:

1. Isaiah 14:13–17
2. John 8:42–47
3. Luke 4:1–13
4. Matthew 25:41–46
5. Revelation 12:1–12

Chapter Four

The Lamb of Trade

"I will bring distress upon the people and they will walk like blind men...
Neither their silver nor their gold will be able to save them..."

Zephaniah 1:17–18

Long before I reach him I can hear his bleating, echoing off the canyon walls around us. The sound is reminiscent of a marketplace, as the hawkers shout about the dull roar of passing shoppers. As my son and I continue climbing, we seem to be getting closer, because now I can begin to distinguish words amidst the clamor. A few moments later, and the words connect into a kind of sing song chant which carries over the mountainside.

> *"Oh who will buy, who will buy?*
> *Take it now and give it a try;*
> *The cost is not much, a pittance indeed, Look in your purse:*
> *you'll find what you need.*
> *Hold it up to the light, see how it glows!*
> *To all who come near, what joy it bestows.*
> *Oh who will buy, who will buy,*
> *This wonderful treasure*
> *come down from the sky."*

When the source of the noise finally comes into view, I'm surprised to see that no one else is around, save a single lamb. He's standing alone, on a level stretch of grass beside the trail. And though he sings of his wares, there are none in evidence. Curious, I draw closer. The lamb doesn't seem to notice me but continues his chant.

> *"Who will buy, who will buy?*
> *I have treasures untold,*
> *Just reach into your purse*
> *And I will consider it sold"*

"What are you selling?" I finally ask as he pauses for breath. The lamb turns to look at me, a smile on his face (if such a thing is possible for an animal). Then the smile fades as he looks beyond where I stand, to my son.

"You don't know?" he asks, still looking past me. "You of all people should know the answer to that." An expression of deep sadness falls over him, and I almost think he's about to cry. But then as suddenly as came, it's gone, and in its place a kind of all-knowing, shared-secret smile. The lamb's eyes meet mine, and all is quiet, as if I'm expected to be the next to speak. The feeling is distinctly uncomfortable, and I look away quickly to clear my throat.

"Well, yes. I suppose I do know what you're selling. And I'm interested, I really am. I don't care about the cost." Now I've said it, and my desperation gives me courage. I return his piercing gaze and utter,

"I just want... it."

"Yes, you do," he smiles. "I can see that. And why not? What could be more precious than a man's own flesh and blood; what price too dear?"

So we understand each other, I think to myself. I need a sacrificial lamb; I can't deny that any longer. Here was a lamb who seemed to know of my mission. Perhaps he was sent by the same One who sent me. "As I said," I began, "I don't care about the cost. Just tell me what it is and I'll get it... somehow."

"A wise man," the lamb announces to the rocks lying about, "a wise man who knows what he wants and will stop at nothing to get it. Truly a wise man. Tell me, wise sir, what have you brought?"

"Only myself, and what few possessions I own," I say as I look around me. "And my son, but..."

"No, we mustn't consider *that* commodity, eh? After all, he's the object of our transaction. Well, let's see..."

The lamb is silent for several moments, considering me as one might consider a middle-aged horse on the auction block. His face clouds over, and I think I can read disappointment in his eyes. My heart floods with despair at the thought that I might not be able to meet the cost.

"If more is required, perhaps I can..."

"Oh have no doubt about that," the lamb cuts me off. "Of a certainty more *will* be required." He examines me thoughtfully again, a low humming sound rising up from deep within him. "I had no idea you were so... deficient." He gives that statement a moment to cut into my heart, then goes on. "But never mind; there are always ways to achieve what one truly desires, eh?"

An electric glow of lightning forms a halo around the summit above, and I'm reminded of the cold altar which waits. I take a step closer to the lamb, my voice shaking in spite of myself. "Could we please go over the terms of the contract? Just so there's no mistake?"

"Oh the agreement is simple enough," he says with a faint air of flippancy. "My life for the life of your son. A fairly easy concept to grasp, when you think about it, although I don't know where you would ever find another so... willing as myself."

A clap of thunder echoes down the canyon, shaking the ground where we stand. The lamb winces and looks quickly toward the source, moving his head from side to side as if trying to peer around the swirling clouds of mist. As he turns to face me, he keeps glancing furtively back over his shoulder.

"At any rate," he continues, "I will fulfill my part of the bargain, but I must have some assurance that you will honor *yours*. After all, the problem of collection will be, shall we say, 'more of a challenge' later on."

At that, a slight hint of a smile seems to return to his face, although I feel like his movements are sharper and more efficient than before.

"But you haven't told me what the price will be. How can I agree to terms when I don't yet know what they are?"

"But you've already said that price is no object." His condemning tone makes me draw back a step. "And I've said that the requirements will not be impossible, only that they will be more than you now possess. I think it's time we concluded this transaction, unless of course you're anxious to meet *Him.*"

Just then, a bolt of lightning splits the sky just overhead. The crack of thunder is instantaneous and seems to originate from within my very soul, knocking me to the ground and paralyzing my senses. As soon as I can recover, I look back toward my son, who incredibly is still on his feet looking up into the clouds. Are those the tracks of a smile on his face?

A clatter of hooves on rocks catches my attention. The lamb is scrambling across the side of the mountain, away from me. The loose shale keeps moving under his feet, sending him sprawling.

"Wait!" I cry out. "We haven't finished the transaction! Come back! Come back! I need you! Don't run away!"

The lamb doesn't answer; he doesn't look back. He just keeps running and falling, running and falling. Finally he reaches an outcropping of rock where he can get a better footing. He pauses for an instant and looks back over his shoulder in my direction. Even from that distance I can see the terror in his eyes. I try to get his attention, but realize he's not looking at me, but rather *around* me: above, below, and on all sides, as if trying to focus on something but unable to do so. Then in the next instant he's gone, out of sight over the ridge.

I fall to my knees in the mud, newly formed by the rain. When did it start raining? Lifting my hands to the sky I cry out, "Why? Why? *Why?* He was going to help me! I was prepared to pay. Please send him back! Please send him back!"

I'm on my face, unaware and unconcerned that the mud and water is coming into my eyes. My nose. My mouth. I lay there for what seems like hours, sobbing at the opportunity lost, then screaming in anger and beating the mud with my fists. Finally, all emotion is drained. I've exhausted every response I know how to express; now there's nothing to do but go on living. As I raise myself up, I notice for the first time that my son is sitting beside me, quietly looking in the direction we have to go. Something is flowing down his cheeks, but whether tears or raindrops I can't tell. We stand up together, and without a word start walking again.

—

It should not have come as any surprise to see the lamb of trade waiting for me on the way up the mountain. From my earliest memories of childhood, I had been taught that the way to success lies in finding the appropriate price for what I wanted and then setting about to meet that price. Did I want a cookie? First I had to say "please," followed by a heartfelt "thank you." It wasn't long before I had mastered this simple transaction, and rarely failed to keep myself as well as my friends supplied with all kinds of treats.

With the coming of age, my taste in treats was broadened, and while the words required to get them became more complicated, the principle remained essentially the same.

"Financial independence" became the ultimate cookie to strive after. I grew old enough to start receiving an allowance, and soon discovered that words were just one way to get what you wanted. Money was the most basic tool, followed by more subtle persuasions, such as influence and power. Even as I began to accumulate wealth in my piggybank, I was being warned of the dangers of these wonderful tools, and I think I responded appropriately. Still, certain realities motivated my life; I wanted to provide myself, my friends, and later, my family with a reasonable standard of living. I wanted to help others less fortunate than myself, and of course I wanted to participate in the American Dream of pursuing at least a few of those "necessities" of life which were paraded in front of me every day. When money or influence was not enough, I soon learned that negotiation would often do the trick.

"I can't pay you $100 today, but I'll give you $10 a month for ten months... oh, eleven months? Okay, it's a deal." Such negotiations were an accepted part of life, and I learned my part well.

It was only natural, then, when my son was first diagnosed with leukemia to ask the obvious questions: what is needed in this situation, and what do I have to do to meet those needs? I'm told this is one of those "man things." Identify the enemy. Seek out and destroy. Medicine was the immediate course of action, and seemed to have a positive effect, at least in the beginning. My wife, too, was more than willing to join in my efforts to find the required payment and appease the Lamb of Trade.

We set out on a fierce program of "positive activity:" vitamins, morning exercises, nutrition, discipline. Maybe if we were just a little more "organized," we thought, we could lick this thing. I'll never forget the night she gave up on the notion. Trevor had been running a low-grade fever at the hospital all day: nothing serious, but annoying, and certainly something capable of defeating. Marsha provided a never-ending stream of liquids, cold compresses and aspirin, all of which Trevor stubbornly refused, distracted as he was by chemotherapy-induced mouth sores. Marsha pushed harder, encouragement moving to suggestion; then cajoling and finally badgering. Trevor, the typical teen, stood his ground until she finally broke down and gave up. She left the room, rather than give him the clear victory, but later returned to confess that she had realized that she could not, by brute force, active will, or extreme organization actuate Trevor's healing. "Super Mom" is a term which loses its luster in the face of such situations.

As the seriousness of the disease became more apparent, however, the questions had to be repeated more forcefully, and more often: *Are* we doing all that is possible to do? *Are* there better medicines available? Are they covered by insurance? What are the limits to my policy? Is this the best treatment centre there is? If another place would offer even one more degree of hope, then I wouldn't hesitate to camp on their doorstep until the required compensation was met.

Gradually, though, it became apparent that whatever the deficiency was, it wasn't monetary. Our mission board's insurance program was the very best money could buy. Even the doctors were amazed to learn how easy it was to get permission for unusual and sometimes expensive treatments. "Do whatever it takes to make him well," they were told. Before several months had passed, more than half a million dollars had changed hands, as one treatment after another was applied. Calls were made to medical centres all over the country, and even in various parts of the world, as the search for clues went out at an increasing rate. Volumes of information were collected and compiled in an attempt to find the hidden formula. I cringed each day as new bills arrived for me to sign and forward on to my mission board. The costs were astronomical; but if that's what it took, then so be it. I'd make it up somehow.

But it was becoming clear to the doctors, if not to me, that something more than financial backing was going to be needed. Nothing was being left undone out of cost considerations. But there was nothing left to do. I refused to accept that conclusion for a long time. *Surely* there were other avenues, other treatments, other places where the answer might be found. I began to pour through medical journals myself, trying to find the missing piece they must have overlooked. But each time I would bring what I thought was "new" information, I would be met with a sigh and the assurance that the information was known to them, but unfortunately it didn't apply to Trevor's case.

Gradually, the truth became clear even to me: money was not going to change things. If I were the richest man in the world, the hospital food might be a little better, but the treatment would be the same. With that realization, guilt swept over me like a flood. What had I done to put ourselves in such a debt of tragedy? If it wasn't money, then *what* did I have to pay? How could I be absolved?

Attitude plays a big part in recovery, I was told. A person who believes he is dying probably will. By contrast, one who refuses to fall into the slough of despond has a good chance of overcoming his malady. If a positive attitude was the key, then I would get it. We began by bringing laughter back into the family, no matter how forced. The local video rental provided hours of entertainment, and we carefully selected programs which would restore our sense of humor. Each day, I would bring the "Far Side" cartoon from the paper; we would look at it together, laugh about it, then tape it to the wall so it could be referred to throughout the day and shared with anyone else who came in. "Calvin and Hobbes" was a favorite, and we enjoyed finding similar situations in our own family, creating our own cartoon panels from real life. Once, the doctor told Trevor he didn't really need anesthetic for his weekly spinal taps; "It builds character," he said with a stern expression. The next day Trevor had drawn an 8 1/2 x 11 figure of Calvin with a horrified expression on his face. The caption underneath read, "*Character!?* Give me *morphine!!*" The medical staff found it so amusing they made several copies of it and distributed it all around the hospital, where we were told that more than a few patients found a reason to laugh that day.

We found more reason to laugh, too, and that was good. Like Julie Andrews, we would spend hours thinking of our "favorite things:" the Japanese food we were missing, old songs, funny incidents, far away friends. It was encouraging to see the "old Trevor" again, with his uncanny sense of finding the humor in any situation. But the bone marrow and the spinal fluid were not impressed, it seemed. Each week, the tests showed either no improvement, or indications of degeneration. Attitude was a powerful tool, but it wasn't the payment I was looking for.

In the midst of my grief, when I should have been closer than ever to the Lord, I found it more and more difficult to carry out even the most basic spiritual tasks which before had been an unquestioned part of my routine. Days would go by without a second glance at my daily Bible reading. Prayer time around the table was a set of rote phrases extracted from the farthest reaches of my mind with no thought given to their meaning. There *were* times of intense supplication, but that's all it was: supplication. Each day sounded much like the day before: "Help me,

Lord. Heal him, Lord. Save us, Lord." If it wasn't obvious to anyone else, it was blatantly clear to me: my life was spiritually bankrupt. Maybe that was the key, I thought. Maybe we're not seeing any improvement because I've yet to meet the minimum requirement for holiness.

The barter mentality within me was awakened, and I set out to get back on the credit side of my spiritual ledger. The Bible was rediscovered and caught up. I made it a point each day to begin with a period of praise, whether I felt it or not. My prayers of supplication were broadened to include someone other than Trevor. A trip to the bookstore yielded a new store of Christian books dealing with everything from personal growth to better evangelism.

Naturally, I knew my own heart, and confessed it to God. All this was motivated by one purpose alone: to see the healing of my son. If I prayed for another, it was because I knew *He* wanted me to pray for another. If I got up an hour earlier than usual to have a time of praise and worship, it was because I knew that's what *He* wanted. Whatever I felt God wanted me to do, I set about to do it with all my strength, if not all my heart. In this way, I hoped, my spiritual bank would be replete, the deficiencies which were holding back God's power would be restored, and my son would recover. I knew the selfish motivation was there, and I knew that God knew it as well. But what was the alternative, I asked? If I can't *feel* like doing what I know I should, then shouldn't I do it anyway, in the hope that feelings will follow? I had always preached this to be true in the case of love. While most of us think of love as an emotion, the Bible teaches that it's an *action*; suitable emotions follow the obedient heart. When Jesus commands us to love our neighbor (Matt. 19:19), He's not demanding some kind of feeling which we couldn't produce if our lives depended on it; He's demanding action appropriate to love. More often than not, when we obey that command and reach out in love to the unlovely, we're surprised to find an accompanying feeling.

In the same way, I felt, obedient response was never wrong, even if the motivations were selfish. After all, wasn't this how children are taught the ways of maturity? When my boys were young, I required that they demonstrated appreciation for every gift they received, even if it was underwear from Aunt Edna. Just as I had been taught to say "please" and "thank you," so they were instructed to say the proper words whether they felt them or not. In the beginning, the words were stilted at best, and often followed immediately with "...but this is not what I really wanted." As the boys grew older, however, the responses became less forced and more automatic. Then one day, it dawned on me that they really *felt* the gratitude they were expressing. In fact I even noticed them teaching younger cousins and friends the same way I had taught them.

So it was not wrong, I was convinced, to work at doing what I felt God wanted me to do, even if I didn't particularly feel like doing it on any given day. As I thought about it, looking at the gospel accounts of the crucifixion, it didn't seem that Jesus Himself especially *felt* like going to the cross on that fateful Friday. He had prayed until sweat drops of blood flowed that some other way be given to accomplish His purpose. What if Jesus had "gone with his feelings" that day? What if He had simply let his heart be his guide, and stood before the Sanhedrin and said, "Nah." That would have been the end of the world as we knew it, and I would not be sitting here today trying to decide if my feelings should dictate obedience.

By the same token then, it was not wrong to force the issue of spiritual obedience, even when I knew that my motivations were anything but pure. Interestingly enough, feelings of commitment did begin to return. Once in a while, I became genuinely concerned for someone other than myself or my family. I began to rediscover the needs all around me: needs which had seemed to slip back into hiding during my dark times. People who had avoided me, or came to offer only the expected words of comfort now shared with me their own battles of the heart. I learned that a friend was facing bankruptcy. Had he not shared that with me before, or had I simply chosen to ignore it in preference to nursing my own hurts? A neighbor's son had committed suicide a short time before I had moved into the house next door. How could I have let this neighbor endure such pain while I sat in my selfish ignorance?

One product of grief, I was learning, was an overpowering urge to retreat within myself. Even though sharing a hurt is the best way to overcome it, that often seems to be the last thing we want to do. There were times when I felt like a prisoner in the dock, as friends would urge me to talk about my pain. I fought it, often violently. But when I finally gave in and started to express those hurts, it got easier. Finally, I came again to the place where I not only wanted to share my own pain, but earnestly desired to hear the pain of someone else's heart. The process was therapeutic, and a good lesson.

With time, I perceived that my spiritual bank was no longer depleted. While selfish motivation started the process, God worked a miracle in my heart to complete it. Eventually, I even remembered why I had begun this program of rejuvenation in the first place: I had been looking for the missing key of recompense, the unpaid debt which left my son's account outstanding. Money was not the problem; I knew that now. A proper attitude helped with the daily challenges of living amidst impending death, but it did not hold the key to recovery. Spiritually, I still went from mountain to valley at the drop of a hat, but I was now convinced that God was requiring from me no more than I had to give.

Finally the night came when all the medicines, all the positive attitudes, all the formulas for success had been depleted. Marsha and I held the body of our son and cried out, "Lord, have we missed anything? Where is the recompense we've been searching for? Would you foreclose on my son's life because of my spiritual poverty? What's left to be paid?"

And in the peace that swept over us, I was convinced that nothing had been left undone. All debts had been paid, and not by my efforts. God had settled accounts long before I was even aware of them. The lamb of trade had tried to convince me that I had been in arrears. With guilt laid upon guilt, he had almost convinced me that I was to blame for my son's death. If I had been more careful, more studious, more prosperous, even more spiritual, all this could have been avoided, he said. Still, there was hope. It might take a lifetime of sacrifice, but maybe, just maybe I could be absolved of my terrible shame, he said.

How many others have fallen victim to this lying lamb's monologue? How many wasted lifetimes have there been of men and women convinced that they have failed to pay the debt of guilt? As far as medical knowledge goes today, I was not responsible for Trevor's death. We don't know what causes leukemia, but it's probably nothing we're doing to our children. Of course that doesn't keep me from speculating, in an endless search for some reason to blame myself. Electric blankets, television sets, computers and prenatal colds have been suggested as contributing factors to this tragic disease, but so far no one has been able to establish a shred of proof.

But what if I *could* point to a cause? What if we discovered that chocolate chip cookies were the culprit? Would that make my guilt any more tangible? What if I had killed my son by a careless act of negligence? Each year, children die in cars driven by their loving parents. Did those parents intend to kill their children? Of course not, but the lamb of recompense is not going to point that out. Some cases are easier for him to try than others, but from the lamb's point of view, *all* are guilty and worthy of the death sentence. And all too often, grieving parents are only too ready to believe it.

When Jesus died for our sins, he died *for our sins*. That means every act of aggression, every slip of the tongue, every careless moment, every step of ignorance. We have no outstanding debts, if we but accept His offer of forgiveness. There are no hidden charges, no taxes, no delivery fees. Fellow climber, if you're counted as a child of God, then you've been given a receipt that says you are debt-free. The next time the lamb of trade confronts you with a new list of charges, just show him that receipt. If you don't happen to have it on you, or if he refuses to look at it, just tell him to address all future correspondence to your Lawyer and Lord. And then rejoice.

For Discussion:

1. What does the term "work ethic" mean? How does that apply to the Lamb of Trade's presentation?

2. Do you believe that some people "deserve" to die while others "deserve" to live? What marks the difference?

3. If you cannot serve God by the proper motivations, is it better then *not* to serve God?

4. When was a time you felt "spiritually bankrupt"? What did you do?

For further study and background:

Look at the parable of the workers in the vineyard (Matthew 20:1–16).

Are you offended or encouraged by the fact that those who came late were still paid the same amount as those who worked all day?

What parallels could you draw between this story and the Christian life?

Chapter Five

The Scapegoat

Aaron shall bring the goat whose lot falls to the Lord and sacrifice it for a sin offering. But the goat chosen by lot as the scapegoat shall be presented alive before the Lord to be used for making atonement by sending it into the desert as a scapegoat.

Leviticus 16:9–10

It's starting to rain. The rumble of thunder in the distance below us announces that more is on the way. Low places in the trail become rivulets of rushing water, making the surface slippery and increasingly more difficult to negotiate. More than once I go down, or else my son loses his footing and lands with a gasp in spite of my efforts to catch him. We're both covered in mud, and I remember another time, centuries ago it seems, when he and I played in a father-son football game. It rained that day too, but we laughed it off, saying that it just made the ground softer to fall on. This time, when we fall, there's no banter, no wise cracks, no comments at all.

In a strange sense, it's almost a relief to fall and lie still for a moment. It's not because we're tired, even though every step seems to take all the strength I can find. I think it's an unconscious delaying tactic, as if by remaining where we fall we can avoid what waits at the top. But each time we eventually stagger to our feet and go on, driven by an urge which we can't explain but which no amount of denial can ignore. The thunder in the darkness below us growls out a warning: whatever waits above is a lot better than what lurks in the shadows below.

The trail works its way around a boulder field, and in one place passes alongside a huge rock which offers some shelter from the rain. We stop for a moment to take advantage of the respite, leaning with our backs against the stone and letting our minds drift in unfocused concentration. Between the darkness and the rain, the surrounding landscape is almost invisible, and yet it's still possible to make out the shapes of boulders all around us. If I was capable of fear at this stage, I could almost imagine them to be living creatures, moving in on us in the night. If this were a 'B' grade movie, I would be close to panic, just about to run blindly into the nothing, until a creature finally caught me and subjected me to a long and cruel death. I say I could "almost" imagine such a scene if I were capable of fear. By now, though, my soul has been drawn and quartered. Nothing from this point on can possibly frighten me... except perhaps what waits at the end of the climb.

I gaze uncaring over the boulder field, and notice something that doesn't belong. Very near. My son sees it too: a vague shape not unlike the surrounding boulders, except that this one is alive. Puffs of condensed air give evidence of breath. Whatever it is, it's not moving, and doesn't seem to be a threat. Our aching muscles are forgotten for a moment, replaced by curiosity, and we edge closer for a better view. Approaching within a few feet, we can see that it's an animal. I take it at first to be a sheep, judging from its size and the hooves, which are illuminated by the occasional flash of lightening. But further inspection reveals a goat, its tiny horns curving around its head to form scythes pointing back toward its eyes. The head is turned in our direction, but it's not looking at us. The eyes draw my attention, if for no other reason than that they draw attention away from his wretched appearance. Beyond the matted hair, the visible ribs, and the uncontrollable shivers, the eyes reflect a hollowness born of despair. There is no light in these eyes, and no indication that they are even capable of seeing.

I motion to my son to move on. This is no animal I want to encounter, talking or otherwise. He may be pitiful, but if I am by now incapable of fear, then I am also incapable of pity. We pass within inches of the creature, and I almost succeed in continuing on without a second glance. But it was the second glance that stopped me cold. Its eyes were now locked onto mine, not in anger nor in fear, but with an expression of pure suffering. I had become a hardened climber, to be sure, but no man could look upon such desolation and not respond. I pause, start to speak, choke for a moment, then manage to utter, "What brings you to this miserable place?"

Even as I ask the question, I'm not sure if I'm referring to the mountain we're on, or to the creature's condition, but he expresses it for me when he answers,

"Nothing brings me here, just as Nothing has brought you here. We are both victims, you and I, victims of false hope in Something, which is really Nothing..."

He hesitates, then shifts his eyes toward my son, and adds, "...all *three of us.*"

I'm struck by the senselessness of his answer, and at the same time angered by the possibility that he might know something of my suffering which I have not been able to comprehend. "What do you mean by 'victims'?" I demand. "I've been brought here for a purpose; one which I detest, but one which nonetheless I must obey. How dare you call our ordeal 'Nothing'?"

"Call it what you may," the goat says in a raspy voice. "But in the end we are nothing more than the sum total of a string of random numbers. Chance has brought me here, and chance has brought you here. If you're trying to find a pattern, a reason, then you're more of a fool than I thought you were."

I stand a little straighter; with one hand gripping my son's shoulder. This creature certainly deserves nothing from me, especially my rage. But this challenge cannot go unanswered. With one hand gripping my son's shoulder, I point with the other in the direction of the goat. "Who are *you* to be talking about chance?" My voice is almost but not quite a shout. "I suppose chance has decreed that you stand there in such a miserable state. Who chose to bring you to this place of death? I suppose you just woke up and found yourself here, looking like a decaying bag of bones. Are you trying to tell me that you had no voice in the circumstances that you've fallen into?"

"Oh I had plenty of voice, all right." For the first time, the goat raises his head, and for a moment I'm struck with a chill which makes me clutch at my collar. Looking me straight in the eye, he continues, "I bleated like there would be no tomorrow when the shepherd grabbed me and the one next to me by the scruff of our necks. And for all we knew, there *would* be no tomorrow. As it turned out, for the other poor soul, our fears were well-founded. Right there, before my eyes, they lifted him up to an altar made of stone and cut his throat. He cried out for as long as he could, but of course that was not for long. His blood poured like a waterfall over the edge of the altar and onto my feet. I was still frozen in shock when the shepherd took a handful of the stuff and flung it all over me."

I notice that the goat is now smiling. He's looking at me until I realize that my hand is resting on my own throat. I drop it to my side quickly and start to speak, but the goat continues.

"Oh yes, there was plenty of chance in force that day. If only I had been feeding at the other end of the trough. If only my head had been lowered instead of raised as the shepherd passed by, perhaps I would have been spared this act of fate."

He looks back at me, and for a moment I catch a glimpse of an expression which at first seems to reflect utter contempt. But then he catches himself, smiles again and looks over at my son while he speaks to me. "Yes, we goats have feelings too. We cry over lost ones. We mourn the various twists of fate which guide our daily paths. We regret what has already become and fear what is yet to be seen."

"But you're not an innocent victim of chance," I insist. "You're the property of a shepherd. What he decides to do with you is his *decision*. It's not some 'twist of fate', as you say. Your life and your death are up to him to administrate. You can't say that 'Nothing' brought you here!"

Now his voice is low, almost a growl, and in the intensity of his words I find myself stepping back in fear. The reaction surprises me. I had thought that fear was a long forgotten emotion, but this creature has succeeded in bringing it back into my face. If he were only threatening pain or loss, I believe I could ignore him. But there was something in his words more sinister, more gut-wrenching than any danger this world might produce: something which he called "Nothing".

"If my life is in the hands of a shepherd, then where is he?" the goat snarls. "You didn't let me finish my story. After the one who was taken alongside me had spilled his blood all over the altar, and me, *I* was carried to the outskirts of the city and driven away, into the wilderness. Driven, do you hear? I tried to go back to my flock, even if it meant back into the arms of that one who had just slit my brother's throat! I bleated, I begged, but they forced me away! They threw rocks at me and kicked at me until I had no choice but to flee into this place of sorry refuge. No, there is no 'guiding hand;' there is no 'master's voice;' there is no 'purpose.' There is only Fate, and it neither smiles nor frowns. It simply *is*."

I feel as if my legs are about to buckle beneath me. My breath is coming in short gasps. I want to deny his words, to stand up to this monster who is turning my world upside down. But I can find no solid ground beneath my feet. Instead I stagger and reel. One arm finds my son's shoulder, and I put my weight upon it. He stumbles, then straightens. Together, we stand and stare at this wretched figure who attacks so cruelly all that has brought us this far. If I too am the property of a Shepherd, can he rightfully kill my son? Can he cast us out into the wilderness like this wretched creature, to die in despair? And what is the alternative? If there is indeed no Shepherd, but only blind chance to direct my life, then what waits for me at the summit? For that matter, what waits for me in the valley below?

The goat seems to have grown larger than before, but I think he's merely standing straighter, losing that first image of abject misery. Now, instead of hollow wretchedness, I can see a barely contained violent rage. The tiny horns which before pointed to hollow eyes now seem to threaten anyone who would dare come near. My newly-rediscovered fear now crumbles into despair and then back to desperation. I can't look away from those eyes.

And then I see it.

Those eyes are not the eyes of one who feels victimized by chance. There's a hatred there which gives the goat strength and purpose. Even hatred must have an object. In spite of what he has told me about the futility of life, his eyes betray a fire which seeks to lash out and destroy. It's a feeling I, too, can share. Just like the goat, I must have something tangible to despise. This goat is not so pitiful, after all. His life began in the hands of a shepherd; now his life is in my hands. Let's see whose he prefers.

I rush toward him. Before he can turn, I grab him by one ear, twist his head to the side and force him to the ground. With a knee firmly in place on his neck, I reach for my knife. The point finds its way just above his jugular vein and I whisper in his ear, "Since you have no hope of altering your fate, then I'm sure you won't complain when I take you to the mountain top with me. My son desperately needs a substitute, and it's going to be you! I would rather present a living sacrifice at the altar, but I'll do what I must to deliver your carcass. Are you coming quietly?"

His eyes, which at first reflected such emptiness and then such hatred now are filled with abject terror. As he struggles, they roll back until only the whites are visible, but even then I can see the fear.

"No!!" he cries. "It isn't supposed to be like this! No! Stop!"

"*Supposed*' to be?" I repeat. "Are you now telling me that there *is* a purpose after all to our misery? Did you have some idea of what our conversation would lead to, and if so, what does that possibly have to do with you?"

—

I don't believe I've ever won a game of chance in my entire life. I *always* landed on Boardwalk when my opponent had put his last hotel in place. In Snakes and Ladders, I was always the one who nearly made it, but landed on a snake at the last minute and had to return to the start. In fact, maybe I shouldn't say I *never* won anything; it might be more accurate to say that I never failed to lose whenever the outcome was left to choice. If I put on a T-shirt in a dark room, I will put it on backwards 100% of the time.

In a way such fortune, or lack of it, is a blessing; I have absolutely no desire to try my hand at the Blackjack table in Las Vegas: the outcome is a foregone conclusion. I don't even bother to scratch the "You could be a winner!" cards you get from petrol stations and fast food restaurants. If in the process I've thrown away a million dollars in unclaimed prizes, that only underscores my point: I'm doomed to lose even when I win. You know those "spot checks" customs officials routinely make at the airport? I'm always the "spot," held up for what seems like hours while every nook and cranny of my luggage is searched for contraband.

I'm not complaining, though, not really. In the first place, it's always an amusing observation to share with friends, and never fails to elicit a certain amount of sympathy. In the second place, in my heart of hearts I know that such an observation is totally without grounds. Contrary to what the heroes of Greek mythology may have believed, there is no "thread of fate" which determines our lives. These ancient tragic dramas would have us think that a man might enjoy a wonderful life, then be struck down for no other reason than that fate had decreed it.

When I think more about it, I suspect that we may find the person we call "unlucky" is in fact deficient in one or more areas, such as coordination, social skills or plain common sense (I could use improvement in all three). The lucky man, by contrast, is perhaps the one who has learned a sense of timing in life which draws him to those right places and right times.

With that philosophy firmly in place, I'm a little taken aback when I see events in the Bible where chance seems to play such an important role. A goat is a goat; I'll grant that, but from the goat's point of view, I might be more concerned if the outcome of a lottery determines whether I'm sacrificed on an altar, or driven into the desert, or left munching my hay. And this is what we see Aaron the priest doing in the sixteenth chapter of Leviticus. Two goats are to be chosen: one for the Lord and one for the scapegoat. The first one is killed and offered as a sacrificial offering while the scapegoat is driven into the wilderness by a man who "stands in readiness" (16:21). By this simple yet powerful ceremony, the people of Israel are given a symbol of their sins atoned for and carried far away. And how were the goats chosen for the task? By lot (16:8).

Before we're too quick to confine the practice of "drawing straws" to the Old Testament, we might want to take a look at the disciples immediately after the Resurrection of Jesus. The church was about to be launched, and the disciples were to be the chosen instruments to get things going. But first they needed to replace Judas Iscariot, who had hung himself (Matt. 27:5). Two men appeared to be likely candidates: Joseph Barsabbas and a man named Matthias. The disciples prayed, then drew lots, and Matthias was the winner (Acts 1:26). Are we to understand from this account that pure chance helped to shape the building of the Church and the men who led it? Or, do we infer that what appears to be chance is not chance at all, but predestined by God, right down to the last straw? I am fully aware that there are some among the readers who follow a particular doctrine, and so already know the answer to that question. Before you skip this section, however, please bear with me. The point I want to make is not so much whether God *creates* those "twists of fate" which direct our daily lives or simply that He *knows* about them in advance and uses them for His glory. I'll leave that discussion to the theologians. What concerns me is this: if the Bible seems to indicate that, at least in some instances the draw of a straw can determine which way I go, then do I have the option of drawing again? If my life is not set in concrete, if I really am a free individual with the ability to make choices which will affect my life, then can I look at a situation and say, "This is not going the way I hoped. Give me some more options, Lord"?

Searching my Bible for any kind of an answer to the mountain of grief that loomed above me, I was struck with the example of the scapegoat. Two goats: one died and one lived, and the determining factor was the drawing of lots. Granted, the goat which was driven into the desert probably didn't have much of a future, separated from all those things which had sustained him up until that time. But if I were given a choice between certain death and probable death, I'd go with the probable every time.

As Christians, we insist that God is not impressed with statistics. That fact certainly held true in the case of my mother, after her heart attack. Her chances for survival plummeted daily, from 50/50 to one in ten, to one in a thousand, to, in the words of one doctor, "not a prayer."

"That's where you're wrong, Doctor," my father was quick to point out. "A prayer is *exactly* what she has, and that's going to make all the difference." And, as you know, it did.

But what about Trevor? Would he be a statistical victim of a disease which at that time and for that variety killed seven out of ten within a year? Or, would prayer make a difference? Would God really intervene and do for my son what He obviously did for my mother? For me, the question of statistics versus faith confronted me daily on the mountain with my son. I *knew* he was in God's hands. I believed that God would heal him... or not, according to His will. But every day I was faced with the responsibility of making decisions about various forms of treatment, and those decisions were shrouded in statistical information which I could not ignore. High dose methotrexate is an effective drug against leukemia, but in about 20% of the cases studied, it gets filtrated into the brain causing severe retardation. "Shall we go with it, Mr. Woods?"

"The tumors are back. More radiation may take care of them, but there's a danger of permanent damage to his central nervous system. Shall we proceed, Mr. Woods?"

"A bone marrow transplant is one possibility, but it's a long shot. Only about 5% of those in your son's condition even survive. What about it, Mr. Woods?"

How would you answer such questions, and by what basis would you arrive at your answer?

Prayer continues to make a difference in my life, and I try daily to remember that God is the author and finisher of all things, and that I am to become neither over despairing nor overconfident at what statistical evidence seems to be showing me. And yet what victims we become! Are we wrong to avoid high crime areas at night because we're more likely to be assaulted there, or should we place complete trust in God and go wherever we wish? Do you wear a helmet when you ride a bicycle because 90% of bicycle fatalities could have been prevented if the rider had worn one, or do you place your life in God's hands and let the breeze flow through your hair?

I know God heals; I've seen Him do so time and again. But in a lot of the cases I've witnessed, He healed through the use of medicine. How do I pick the right medicine, and when do I say, no more? When do I simply trust God for a miracle, as some of my brothers and sisters in the Lord would have done from the very beginning, eschewing medicine altogether? At this juncture, what I'm really saying is, "Where is the scapegoat?"

The example of the scapegoat seems to be telling me that there are alternatives in life. Two goats were chosen: one died immediately while the other was driven into exile. If my sin is represented in those goats, then is my life also illustrated in their fate? Both ultimately died, and I must accept the fact that I too as a son of Adam have an appointment with death which I cannot escape (Heb. 9:27). I cling to the assurance, and find joy in the fact that my sin has been carried away once and for all by the Lamb of God, and I need fear neither the altar nor the desert. But as certainly as sin remains in the world today, my life is going to be affected by its scars. The mother of the illegitimate child can be forgiven for her action, but nevertheless that child has been created in the process, and will bring all the challenges and responsibilities which follow. The young man who spent his college years "tripping out" on drugs may come to his senses as an adult, but he or his children may still suffer the residual effects for years to come. You or someone you know may very well have suffered a disability from birth, and while the exact cause may not yet be completely understood, it's generally accepted that something in a previous generation went terribly wrong, and the scars are evident today. Someday, we may learn the causes of leukemia and how to prevent it, but in the meantime we must move forward with what information we have, and with God's leading hope for the right choices.

Did my son have a choice? Did I make the right ones for him? Was he merely a statistic, or a victim of fate? I sincerely look forward to learning the answers to those questions someday, when God will wipe away all our tears. But until then I will continue to be faced with decisions, and it gives me some comfort to know that I am a part of a distinguished company of decision makers. Throughout the Bible's history, men have been called upon to exercise their freedom of choice. "Choose for yourselves this day whom you will serve," said Joshua to the chosen ones, then went on to declare, "But as for me and my household, we will serve the Lord" (Josh. 24:15). Joshua's decision to take the Lord's side brought him blessing and a place among the saints. To have chosen otherwise would have undoubtedly led him to disaster.

Martha's sister Mary was faced with the choice of attending to the household work or attending to Jesus. Martha criticized her for her decision, but Jesus affirmed her, saying that "Mary has chosen what is better, and it will not be taken from her" (Luke 10:42).

Paul had to decide between life and death, and considering the persecution he was experiencing at the time, the choice was not an easy one to make. When he wrote to the Philippian church about his difficulties, he was not speaking symbolically. "I am not sure which I should choose. I am pulled in two directions. I want very much to leave this life and be with Christ, which is a far better thing; but for your sake it is much more important that I remain alive" (Phil. 1:22–24).

Reading the testimonies of men and women such as these, I am led to believe that choice is an essential part of our lives. Alternatives not only exist, but the choice of one alternative over another can have eternal impact on a person. God may know which choice we will make, but the choice is still ours. As John writes, "Whoever *chooses to believe* on him shall not perish but have everlasting life" (John 3:16).

In the matter of scapegoats, the question presents itself: are there alternatives to circumstances, and how can we choose them? Ezekiel quotes God as looking for someone to "stand in the gap before me so that I would not destroy" (Ezekiel 22:30). May this Scripture be taken as an application for other situations? If so, then does that mean that one person might actually prevent the destruction of another by coming before God on his behalf? In the midst of my grief, not wishing to leave any stone unturned, I took this idea before the Lord. "If someone must die of leukemia, then I pray that it would be me," I pleaded. "Take the curse from my son and place it on his father. I willingly accept whatever you decree in order that my son live."

More than anything else, I wanted to be the scapegoat for Trevor. What a glorious thing, to sacrifice one's life for his son! The thought permeated my mind, and for awhile I waited expectantly to see if God would approve the choice. If I started showing signs of cancer, then I would rejoice, since it would mean that my son would live. To my great disappointment, nothing happened except that Trevor continued his slide, and I was left to reexamine the role of the scapegoat.

As in the original meaning of the word, in more recent times, we've come to use the term "scapegoat" to describe anyone who "takes the rap" for another, usually against his will. The "rap," as far as Israel was concerned, was their problem of sin. With no hope for forgiveness outside of the Law, the only hope was for absolute compliance. The Torah, which we identify as the first five books of the Old Testament, was quite explicit in describing the bare minimum of obedience required to God. Everything from the proper treatment of livestock to responsibility to family to the acceptable forms of worship was spelled out in detail. The people tried... and failed. Then they tried again... and failed again. Prophets followed prophets with warnings and declarations. Israel slipped into a time of despair when every man did what was right in his own eyes (Judges 17:6). More prophets followed, along with "judges", and then finally, God was quiet. For four hundred years, in the time known as the "intertestamental period", Israel suffered in the knowledge that they had fallen short. Even a cursory glance through the Torah would be enough to demonstrate that unrighteousness had not only survived, but had "increased" (Rom. 5:20). Like it or not, sin was a grim reality, made more grim by the reminder that "without the shedding of blood, there is no remission of sin." (Heb. 9:22). The blood sacrifice was necessary to drive home the seriousness of rebellion. Just as God killed animals to provide clothes for the "enlightened" Adam and Eve (Gen.3:21), man ever since has needed a visual lesson in the wages of sin. Not until an Israelite actually watched an animal die, its blood running off the altar gathering around the base, and then was reminded that *sin* made such a gruesome spectacle necessary, was he finally able to comprehend what it means to reject his Creator. I'm truly glad that such things are no longer necessary, but at times I think we all could use a good dose of reality now and then: to observe first hand what happens as a direct result of our own personal sin. It would not be a pretty sight, but perhaps it would cause me to hesitate the next time I'm tempted to go against those laws which God established for my good.

But even death and shed blood was not enough to illustrate the severity of the situation to Israel. Another goat was required, one that would not die at once but would be driven away from the flock, out of the city, into the desert, there to die alone, uncared for and unmourned. What more appropriate picture of the sacrifice to come, when the Lamb of God would follow in the model set so many years before. The prophet Isaiah was given a picture of a time which, mercifully, he would not see with his own eyes. And yet as we read his words, one cannot help but feel the torture this man of God was experiencing when he tried to recount the vision:

He was despised and rejected by men, a man of sorrows, and familiar with suffering. Like one from whom men hide their faces he was despised, and we esteemed him not. Surely he took up our infirmities and carried our sorrows, yet we considered him stricken by God, smitten by him, and afflicted. But he was pierced for our transgressions, He was crushed for our iniquities; The punishment that brought us peace was upon him, and by his wounds we are healed. We all, like sheep have gone astray, each of us has turned to his own way; and the Lord has laid on him the iniquity of us all.

(Isaiah 53:3–6)

With this tragic, yet magnificent picture before us, the image of the scapegoat becomes more than simply a *substitute* for sin. By its very nature, the scapegoat *becomes* the sin. Although I desperately wanted to fill the role, Trevor did not need a scapegoat, because the issue of guilt had already been settled on Calvary.

One night as he lay in bed, unable to sleep for the relentless pain which racked his body, he turned and asked, "Dad, am I being punished?"

"Of course not," I was quick to reply. "God doesn't work that way. Do you feel guilty?"

"No, I guess not. But I've done some things I'm not too proud of." And at that point, he proceeded to confess all the sins he could think of, as well as a few he had considered but never had the time or opportunity to follow through on. I wasn't too impressed with his list, especially compared to my own "guilt closet" I maintain for those special times when I like to feel sorry for myself. But to Trevor, this was a serious issue, and I treated it as such.

"Have you asked God to come into your heart?"

"Of course, Dad, don't you remember? I was nine years old, and you baptized me yourself!"

"Do you remember what you said in front of the church?" In Japanese churches, every new Christian must write a statement of faith, which is approved by the membership before baptism. The statement then goes into a permanent church file.

"Not exactly. I was just a kid."

"You said, 'Jesus lives in my heart now, and He's forgiven me for all the bad things I've done.' Do you think you've done anything since then that's too bad for Jesus to forgive?"

"No, I guess not. But why is this happening to me?"

"I don't know, Trevor, but I can tell you this: it's not happening because you've been bad. When God forgave you, He put all your sin so far away, even *He* can't remember it. You're not being punished, and don't forget it."

Suddenly, my case for wanting to be Trevor's scapegoat went out the window. A scapegoat carried away a person's sins. Trevor had no unforgiven sin, so a scapegoat would be redundant. There was nothing I could do in the area of sacrifice that had not been done already.

If I couldn't find a scapegoat, then neither could I blame my troubles on fate, as the example of Aaron shows us. *Both* rams he chose were symbolic of the sins of the people; both were sacrificed: one on the altar, one in the desert. The reason two were used was for the simple fact that one could not serve both purposes. You can't kill a goat, then drive it into the desert. Driving it away first, then bringing it back to kill it seems to lose something of the symbolism. Two goats were used because two were required. Casting lots was as good a method as any for selecting the scapegoat, since the fate of both was to pay the price of sin.

Later of course, the Perfect Sacrifice was able to fulfill both roles completely. He was despised and rejected *and* slain for our sin. I had no hope of substituting for either ram, and since such a substitution was no longer required, I had no need to do so.

—

The goat hesitates, until I draw the knife closer to his throat, then screams out, "It wasn't me! He told me to meet you. He said you'd give up the journey. He said all you needed was a little case of despair. It's not my *fault*," he whimpers. "Please let me go!"

The miserable creature is almost at the end of his strength. Just another fraction of pressure and I could end his pitiful bleating. But as I look up at my son, then down at the goat, I realize that this defective object will never suffice for a substitute. Standing up, I resist the urge to kick him away. Instead I turn my back to him and cry, "Get out of here. Tell your master you've failed. Let him decide what your *fate* will be."

At first the goat is silent, as if weighing his

alternatives, then with a sigh, he rises and moves backwards. He leaves slowly at first, until I turn back to face him; then he begins to clamber down the mountainside. I'm surprised to see such speed and agility in one who seemed so wretched. In another moment, he's gone. The adrenaline has left me as well, and I collapse to the ground, sobbing. I almost believed him. I came so close to falling into a pit from which there could be no rescue, for in its depths there is no hope of a shepherd.

Finally I can rise, and together we move on toward Something.

For Discussion:

1. Do you believe God *creates* your circumstances, or uses them to accomplish His purpose?

2. If God is the Master of circumstance, then are seatbelts, helmets and safety glasses really necessary?

3. Would you be willing to "stand in the gap" (Ezekiel 22:30) for the sake of someone else? What are ways you might do this?

4. How does your family make important decisions? What do you think of the disciples' method of praying, then drawing straws (Acts 1)?

For further study and background:

Look through the Bible's examples of the sacrificial system. Why do you think it was important to witness such a barbaric spectacle? Consider these verses as you study:

Genesis 3:21
Exodus 5:17
Exodus 13:15
Exodus 20:24
2 Kings 17:35

2 Samuel 24:24
Psalms 51:16
Malachi 1:8
Matthew 9:13
Romans 12:1

Chapter Six

The Magician's Lamb

Keep on, then, with your magic spells and with your many sorceries, which you have labored at since childhood. Perhaps you will succeed; perhaps you will cause terror.

Isaiah (Isa. 47:12)

The trail grows narrower as we approach the summit. A series of switchbacks tells us that our progress is still upward, but also providing us with opportunity for rest at each turn. We're gaining height quickly now, evident by the fact that the air has taken on a thin quality. Breathing is more difficult, and my son is wheezing with every step. I want to do something to help him, but there's not a thing I can think of. It's colder, I notice. There's a sharp sensation all about, as the cold settles around us, working its way through my clothes and finding the inner reaches of my very heart. I pull up my collar, but it does nothing to drive out the chill.

My thoughts drift back to warmer times. Days on the beach. Afternoons on the job. The heat then was either welcome or not, but it was always something which was simply *there*. I remember my scientist uncle asking me a question once, when I was about nine years old. "Tell me this," he said, "is heat the absence of cold, or is cold the absence of heat?" I had no idea, so he answered the question for me. "Heat is something you add to a situation to make it hotter," he explained." There's no such thing as a 'cold source'; therefore, heat is artificial, while cold is just the way things are without it." I reminded him of freezers, refrigerators and air conditioners, but my uncle said simply, "All those things do is remove heat." I wasn't able to fully understand the concept back then, and I'm not even sure I do now. But what I do know is this: in the absence of heat on this mountain, every fiber of my being is missing it, and longing desperately for anything which would bring even a measure of relief.

We stop for a moment to blow into our hands and slap at our arms to try and restore circulation. As I look around me, the landscape on this mountainside seems so dark, so devoid of anything alive. And that figures, I suppose. The only living things we've seen since the light faded were a lamb and a goat, and now that I think of it, I'm not even sure *they* were alive; not really. Why is it that darkness and death go hand in hand? Is that why dead people are supposed to have their eyes closed? And by the same token, if a dead person has his eyes open, there's something unnatural about it: even unexplainably frightening. When God assured Jacob that his son Joseph would "close his eyes" (Gen. 46:4), He was surely telling him much more than the simple fact of his death. A dead man with open eyes is lacking completion, resolution. God promised Jacob that his own son would provide that for him.

I wonder who will close my eyes?

Standing there in the darkness, shivering not just from the cold, it feels like I'm in the very presence of Death itself. Am I anticipating what lies ahead, or has Death already begun to surround us, its icy fingers gripping our throats as we struggle for each breath?

Moving around, stamping my feet, trying to generate even a tiny bit of heat, I've gradually become aware that the atmosphere surrounding us has begun to change. I might even imagine that there's a certain measure of warmth in the air; maybe not so much *warm* as perceptibly not as cold as before. Either way, I turn in the direction of the change. My senses are pricked as I seek out what offers a vague promise of relief. There it is again: a definite presence, not as cold as the surroundings, carried by the wind and wrapping itself around me. I step off the trail and move around a large boulder which is blocking what little view I can make out in the darkness. The journey to the top can wait until I locate the source of this warmth. Coming to the other side of the rock, I see another lamb, facing away from me. Right away, it's obvious that this is not a pitiful creature like the scapegoat was. This animal seems well-fed and strong, as if he has been cared for. His strength appeals to me in a cruel sort of way. Knowing that with each step up this mountain I am becoming more and more wretched, my soul longs for something which is thriving. The lamb has his nose down, almost touching something which rests at his feet. I move closer for a better view, and I can see the object which is the focus of his attention. It seems to be a piece of coal, or something very similar. The object is black, about the size of a large grapefruit, and while there's no glow about it, still it seems to be radiating some kind of heat. The lamb is studying this phenomenon, not moving a muscle. I wonder if it knows I'm standing here.

Just then, the lamb speaks.

"There is power in this place," he says in a voice that is nearly trance-like. "Mortal man cannot know the width and breadth of it; but with guidance, he may discover its depth."

The statement is meaningless to me, but somehow I feel that it's *supposed* to be, as if the saying of it is more important that what's actually said. Rather than dwell on it, I draw closer instead to the black object which holds such a fascination. "What is it?" I ask in a whisper, as if it might disappear if I were to approach too suddenly.

"The question of the ages." He says, as though reciting a poem. "Standing at the portals of Knowledge, man can only wonder what lies beyond. Will he ever know the answer to the riddle?" The lamb turns and looks straight through me. "Will *you?*"

"I want to know," I answer, as a stirring of hope pushes me forward. I want badly to reach out and touch the black object, to feel its warmth and test its weight. Something inside me is warning me to back away, but the desire to *know* is too great. I push aside my fear and speak up again, "I want to know. If there is power, then I want to have it. Can you help me?"

The lamb seems to think a moment, staring off into the darkness. Is he looking at someone? I strain my eyes in the same direction, but I can't see anything. Finally, as if some kind of order has been issued, his body tenses for a moment. Then he seems to relax, and he turns to face me. "Yes, I can help you. I see that you have a heart to seek out what was forbidden. You are a warrior, and will not be prevented from winning what is rightfully yours." The lamb takes two steps backwards, watching me the whole time. I'm not surprised when he says, "Pick up the token."

Without asking, I know already what he's talking about. The black object seems to be even warmer as I stare at it. There's still no glow to be seen; not even a trace of light escapes from it. But the heat *is* there. And where there's heat, there's power: power to warm the body, power to control. Perhaps there is even power to heal. I take a deep breath and reach out slowly with both hands, ready to grab it quickly if it tries to escape, or if someone else should dare to try and take it. As if for approval, I steal a quick glance in the direction of the lamb. He's not looking at the object which so rivets my own attention; I notice. Instead, he's looking at me. The thought crosses my mind that the lamb knows already what the black object will or will not do. But he's not so sure yet about me. His mouth is hanging open, and from the tiny puffs of condensed air, I can see that his breathing is coming in short bursts between long periods of absolute stillness. I hesitate. Just what does he expect to happen when I grab hold of this thing?

"Why do you wait, Mortal One?" he says in a voice that fairly bursts with anticipation. "The key to your quest lies within your grasp. It is yours. Take it."

I move a step closer, presumably to place my feet in a better position, but actually to gain a moment to think. Is this really the object of my search, or is it yet another trap? The lamb of anger had tried to make me curse God and bring about my own harm, while the scapegoat had almost convinced me to turn back from the journey. What is this... this *magician* trying to do? Maybe I should I grab the lamb instead, I think to myself. Maybe *he's* the real source of power that I'm looking for. Perhaps it's only my imagination, but the black object almost seems to be humming in anticipation, demanding every thought I hold except the thought of holding *it*. It takes a conscious effort of will, but I manage to tear my eyes away from the object and look instead at the lamb. Suddenly, his expression changes, and he takes a step in my direction. Where before he seemed to hold the wisdom of the ages, now I can see real fear in his eyes.

"What are you doing?" he asks, his cracking voice revealing the turmoil inside. "Are you mad? Take the token! Take the token!"

"What is the token?" I ask. "What will I have to pay to take it?"

"Those are the questions of a *fool*," he sneers. "Do you think such an opportunity comes to every mortal, and more than once in a lifetime? This is your *chance*. Think of your son!"

The lamb makes a quick glance upward, toward

the top of the mountain, then turns back to me and continues, "Think what *He* will do when He gets his hands on that one you love so much!"

At any other time a statement like that would have urged me to action. But I've heard those words before, and not very long ago. I have to stop a moment and think: why are these creatures so concerned about *Him*? Is it in fact really me they want to help, or are they plotting against Him?

The lamb can see that my mind is backing away, and the fear that he was feeling is now exploding into rage. "Mortal!" he screams. "You have no more right to *real* power than your son has! Now *both* of you will live to regret your mistakes. Taste the bile of fear. Let it lie in your throat, until your miserable life is choked away from you!"

With a sudden movement, the lamb lunges at me, the top of his head connecting with one leg and pushing me off balance. I start to fall, and instinctively throw out my left hand to meet the ground. But instead of stone, my hand lands on the black object. The pain of a thousand burning needles pierces through my palm and shoots upward until my entire arm is in agony. I roll off to one side, clutching my hand and screaming in agony. "Oh God! It hurts!"

The cry was not meant to be directed at Anyone in particular, but it was heard. There's a change in the atmosphere, like the static charge that builds just before a lightning strike. The lamb, which had been standing over me with a vicious grin on its face now freezes. We both remain motionless, scanning our surroundings. The silence is almost deafening. I'm about ready to try and stand, in order to look behind me when the world turns upside down.

From somewhere beyond the rock which lies between us and the trail, there comes an ear shattering roar. The ground shakes and I'm tossed around, totally helpless. I may be screaming, but if I am, it's insignificant to the sound which fills the night. When I finally regain my balance and sit up, I'm face to face with the lamb. His eyes are turned upward until only the whites are visible. Then as I try to comprehend what has just happened, the lamb raises his head to look higher still, over my head and behind me. An expression of sheer terror falls on him like a net, and he starts backing away.

"No!" he cries. "I've done nothing wrong! *He* asked me! *He* wanted it! Let me go!"

I struggle to twist around, and turn my head in the direction of the rock, an unspoken terror filling my own heart at what I might see. There, in the twilight over the stone, I can see nothing; at least nothing I can perceive with my eyes. I look back at the lamb, but he's still staring up at the space over the rock and backing away, all the while screaming out his innocence. Then he goes quiet, as if struck dumb by some unseen force. He remains still and quiet for perhaps a full minute, then turns and runs, leaping over a ravine and disappearing from sight in a matter of seconds. I look again back behind me and still can not see what has terrified him so. Rising to my feet, I rub my injured hand; I'm surprised to discover that it no longer hurts.

My son is kneeling near the spot where we had first seen the lamb. I manage to move closer to him before my legs give way and I collapse at his side. "Ashes. Nothing but ashes," he says softly.

My eyes follow his to the spot where the black object had sat, radiating what I thought had been heat, but which in fact was only a lesser degree of cold. There in a neat pile, lay what was left of the object: coal black ashes, without a trace of warmth in them. My son bends lower and blows on them. In an instant they're gone, spread into the darkness. "Ashes," he repeats.

There's nothing else to keep us here. We stand together and return to the rock and beyond, to the trail that waits for us.

—

It has always seemed rather strange to me that the magician never shows himself to those of us he wants to control. He would have me believe that I'm fortunate indeed not to have had the experience. Coming face to face with the magician, I'm told, would so fill me with terror that I would be instantly and completely reduced to a blubbering idiot. It's certainly true that man's attempts to imagine what the magician looks like have resulted in some pretty awesome pictures. Those grotesque, inhuman yet horribly *humanoid* creatures with the reptilian skin and venomous eyes are enough to make any of us back away from the threat of the magician's power; and yet what are they, really, but images of our own making, put together by the God-given mystery we call our minds?

I strongly suspect that the magician himself is somewhat less the imposing figure than we would make him out to be. And because that's true, he prefers to send his agents as stand-ins against us: creatures which do possess a limited power of deception but which at the bottom line are nothing more than creatures, bankrupt of any real power. And when you think of it, even what power they profess to have is doomed to destruction because of Calvary. Jesus Himself reminded Pilate that "You would have no power over me unless it was given you from above (John 19:11). There is, in fact, no magic wand, no enchanted formula, no "black orb" which can deliver power beyond what God has allowed. And so, like the Wizard of Oz, the magician locks himself behind fortified emerald walls of deception, amplifying his voice over the terrified citizens and projecting images of a godlike figure. And of course, that is exactly what he wants to be but never will.

Over the centuries since his banishment from Paradise, the magician has developed quite a following, both from the seen as well as from the unseen world. Cast out of the Kingdom because of their foolishness, this band of rebels has made it their stated purpose to usurp the Creator and replace Him with a created being, namely the magician himself. Such a task is of course ludicrous, and the magician has no more hope of gaining such a position of authority than does the scab on my knee. But you have to concede him this much: he knows success when he sees it.

Whenever he can, and to whatever extent he is allowed, the magician has tried to copy the Creator's work in order to accomplish his own miserable ends. When Moses called upon the Creator's power to transform a staff into a snake (Exodus 7 ff), the impostor said, "Oh yeah? I can do that!" and proceeded to come up with a couple of pretty decent copies for his own priests. Never mind that they were summarily devoured by the Creator's staff/snake; the effect was good.

A few thousand years later, we see the magician still at it. The Creator's Son had told the world that He had come to "bind up the broken hearted" and to "restore sight to the blind" (Isaiah 61, Luke 4). From out in the darkness, we hear, "Oh yeah? I can do that!" and from the mist emerges nothing less than a lamb: a gentle looking creature with an expression of harmony and a heart for healing. At first, he is rejected in much the same fashion as the Creator's Son was: man has wallowed in his own mire for so long, any resemblance of mercy is taken for a poor joke. But then the magician's lamb does something absolutely incredible:

He heals people.

For anyone even faintly aware of events in the world today, it should come as no great surprise to discover that God's power is not the only power at work around us. Of course we have to understand that

God, as Creator, has brought all things into being. There are no other creators around, and so ultimately we will have to acknowledge that all power belongs to Him. But that does not eliminate the possibility that certain portions of God's creation have been twisted and used for purposes for which they were never intended. We don't have to look far to see that things like sex and appetite have been grossly mishandled until these gifts are routinely associated with evil, rather than the good they were created to be. Power itself has demonstrated more than once to be absolutely corrupting in the hands of the corrupted. Where many of us fall into deception, however, is in the assumption that "good power" always looks like "good power," and by the same token, "bad power" will never fail to look evil. Maybe television sitcoms are largely to blame, or maybe it's just our own tendency to want to simplify an otherwise complicated concept. Whatever the source, it seems that it just hasn't occurred to many of us that all those "good" looking things out there are not necessarily what they appear to be.

Actually, when you think about it, isn't it true that virtually all of us, from childhood, have been trained to appreciate all those "good" forces out there regardless of their origin? Let's go back to the Wizard of Oz. If I remember correctly, the whole affair began when Dorothy inadvertently landed her house on the bad witch of the north, incurring the wrath of her sister. But not to worry: the plucky girl from Kansas was finally rescued and brought home again, thanks to the leading of the good witch of the south.

Of course we all cheered when Cinderella's fairy godmother stepped in to change her life with a little magic. Those step sisters of hers were not only wicked; they were *ugly*! Cinderella deserved a break, and if it took an enchanted pumpkin, a few white mice and a glass slipper to save the day, then let's hear it for fairy godmothers.

And who didn't smile when the puppet Pinocchio was given the gift of life: to be made into a "real live boy"? For him, it seems, flesh and blood existence depended on nothing more than clean living, a real encouragement for those children who regard themselves as "good". Pity the one who falls short of the mark, but that's another story.

Sleeping Beauty's curse, put upon her by a jealous witch, was finally ended by nothing more spiritual than a handsome prince's kiss, and the back of the Imperial Storm Trooper was broken by the power of the Jedi Knights, welded together by the omnipresent "force".

While a child will eventually grow beyond a belief in fairies and witches, inside most of us something is left behind; a kind of hope that, just maybe, there *are* forces of good pitted against those forces of evil which generally make our lives miserable. "Yes, Virginia, there *is* a Santa Claus." Even (or perhaps especially) as adults, we yearn for something beyond ourselves which would take the ugliness in and around us and turn it into something beautiful. Is it possible that we yearn for something which was once ours, but has been lost?

In fact, there was once a time when hope was in full bloom, as was the rest of the Garden. Creator met with His created in a relationship of pure joy. Work was meaningful, and pleasant. Love was an emotion to be cherished, not sought after. The future held no fear: what could possibly be feared when the Master Himself held the future in His hands?

But there was reason to be afraid, and the reason was within the heart of Man. Real love could not be genuine without the freedom to withhold it. The tree in the garden, the one called the tree of the Knowledge of Good and Evil, was the symbol of that freedom. Of course, it didn't have to be a tree; it could just have easily have been a park bench with a sign over it saying "Don't sit here." Man had to have something by which he could express his love for God, free of any restraint. Anything would do, as long as a man could come before it and say, "Because I love my Creator, I choose to do his bidding, either by carrying out the tasks He gives me, or by refraining to do what He has told me not to do." The symbol of obedience was the tree, and it wasn't long before both the man and the woman demonstrated a rebellious heart, pushed into action by the deceptive work of the enemy.

In the years since that time, separated from the Garden and from that face-to-face relationship with his Maker, Man has floundered time and again, wandering farther and farther from what he wants most: to return to the way it was. Deep within each of us, there lies a memory. Just as something drives the migratory birds to risk life itself to return to a place they've never known; just as the spawning salmon will stop at nothing to reach the place of its birth before it gives up its life, so it is with Man. We've been driven from the Garden, but a part of the Garden remains inseparably a part of us. The hardest of men, in times of honest introspection, will recall a time and a place when life was pure and holy; and if he's honest with himself he'll look with longing on those days, yearning to be free of the emotional baggage which has made his life the burden it's become.

Jesus understands that longing. How His heart must have ached in the synagogue of Nazareth when he opened the scroll of Isaiah and read to the people who had been so close to Him as He grew up:

The Spirit of the Lord is on me, because he has anointed me to preach good news to the poor. He has sent me to proclaim freedom for the prisoners and recovery of sight for the blind, to release the oppressed, to proclaim the year of the Lord's favor.

(Luke 4:18–19)

He knew very well that man had become poor: made destitute by generation after generation of looking in all the wrong places. He knew that the freedom which was so necessary to genuine love had been the instrument of man's bondage, and to man's blindness, and to man's oppression at the hands of the enemy of God. Even the act of proclaiming the long-awaited year of the Lord's favor upon man didn't remove at once the chains that held him so tightly. Instead, the telling of the Good News brought a reaction of wrath upon the Son Himself. Jesus suffered in his soul at the sight of what Man had become. But He also rejoiced at the knowledge of what Man would once again be. As His disciples first began to explore the depths of long-forgotten joys, reporting back to the Son that "even the demons submit to us in your name" (Luke 10:17), Jesus shared their delight and rejoiced with them over the coming defeat of spiritual blindness. "Blessed are the eyes that see what you see," He said. "For I tell you that many prophets and kings wanted to see what you see but did not see it, and to hear what you hear but did not hear it" (Luke 10:23–24).

But not everyone has been so blessed. Because the restoring of sight requires free and uncoerced acceptance on the part of the blind, many still grope in darkness, looking for the light, but refusing to reach out to the Source that stands just outside the heart. Instead, Man stumbles in the darkness, seeking a way, *any* way but the Only Way which will lead him to wholeness.

The enemy can't know the hearts of men as Jesus does, but he's no fool. He's quick to recognize that desire for restoration in the gropings of men and he's only too willing to offer hope, however unfounded. Rather than offer a blatant lie, which would be rejected out of hand, he plays to the ray of hope left over in every human heart.

"Yes," he acknowledges, "you *are* hurting. You *have* lost your way. You've made a mess of things, and you know that there's no way you can possibly make it right in your own strength."

So far, he has spoken the truth, and Man listens. Then the enemy goes a step farther.

"Look around you," he says, "surely you can see that there is power to be incorporated. This world is not simply what we see. There are realms beyond your sight which men can only dream of."

Once again, the deceiver has depended on truth to establish his authority. Man listens, and nods in agreement. The knife is set, and now the blade is turned.

"How can you apportion this power for yourself?" the enemy asks the rhetorical question, and then answers it.

"*I* can lead you. Come with me."

At that point, truth becomes deadly lie, and rather than being freed of his blindness, Man is pulled even farther into the dark. One step at a time, he's convinced that power is available outside of the Creator of all power. Without the restrictions associated with obedience, he comes to believe that Forces other than God are available to him.

The real tragedy is that there *are* forces available to him: forces which may not necessarily appear at first to be harmful. In the final analysis, though, they will rob the man of his freedom, his dignity, his life, and even his very soul: all the while appearing as an angel of light, bringing healing, wealth and fulfillment of every heart's desire.

As Trevor's pain increased, it became more and more obvious that he was in need. Medicine could only go so far in relieving the agony, and our prayers, in as far as we understood, seemed to be having very limited effect. The enemy had a golden opportunity, and he made the most of it. Almost daily, for a period of several weeks, we were bombarded with offers of help from well-meaning, and I believe sincerely motivated individuals. First came the New Age disciples. Healing was a matter of mind over body, we were told. The powers of the mind were beyond our comprehension, but not beyond our control. Social workers and hospital "chaplains" came to Trevor's bedside to offer what they called "meditations" designed to line up the adverse forces surrounding him. A dear friend brought a crystal she had purchased for a substantial price and asked him to wear it. The forces which it concentrated, he was told, would combat the pain and even heal the leukemia if he would give it enough time. A nurse would come into his room on her own time in order to sit by his bed and focus her own energy with his, thereby defeating the harmful emanations.

We couldn't help but appreciate the love and desire for relief which the efforts of these people demonstrated. Without calling down fire on their heads for their blasphemy, we told them in no uncertain terms that there was only one Physician on Trevor's case, and any healing of a spiritual nature would have to come from Him. Eventually, they got the message, and their visits gradually stopped. But the testimonies they left behind continued to echo about the room. The boy down the hall was healed after a concentrated meditation session. A girl who wore a crystal had now gone home, apparently free of the cancer which had brought her there. It was hard to hear of such "successes" and not wonder, "Am I doing the right thing?" Watching my son writhe in agony on his bed as one medication after another was tried with no effect, I had to ask myself, "*Are* there other methods which would work? Could I justify using them? Where does experimental medicine leave off; where does blind faith come to an end and acknowledgment of demon powers begin?"

We were in the States at the time of Trevor's illness, but even there the influence of Japan's spiritual bondage was made evident. A friend sent me a book about "Mahikari", a spiritualist approach to healing which tries to focus one's power into the palm of the hand and thus outward to the sick and injured. Buddhist and Shinto followers from all over the country, friends and associates whose concern for Trevor was unmistakable but whose gods were not my God, wrote and called to say that they were praying for healing.

I was touched by their obvious love for us, but the touch brought another, colder contact. The powers of this world were hard at work, in an attempt to take credit for what God was about to do. Already, they had convinced many that any good which came about would be from those powers, apart from any such thing as "faith" or "Providence." I had to wonder: do these powers have the ability to work miracles? It was certainly hard to deny that many apparently wonderful things had happened immediately after some requirement was met which had nothing to do with faith in God. Where were the limits to their power? How could I refuse sincere offers of help for my son, even if those offers involved a faith which I didn't share?

One thing which helped me put the problem into perspective was remembering the words of consolation I heard often from my boss when I was working summer jobs on a construction project. Every time I'd hit my finger with a hammer, or crack my head on a beam, he'd smile and say, "Just think how good that's gonna feel when it quits hurting!" For some reason, I *was* comforted by those words. Later, as the sharp pain would recede into a dull throb, and finally when rubbing the sore spot brought genuine pleasure, I had to admit, "This feels good!" Never mind that the good I felt was in contrast to the agony which it had replaced. There seems to be a comparison here to the work of the devil. If Satan can persecute me (and the Bible seems to indicate that he can), until I'm just about ready to despair, then when he backs off, how do I feel? I feel *great*! To be rid of the persecution is almost as good a feeling as I had before the persecution ever started: maybe even more so, since I now appreciate the freedom from it. By the same token, I can testify to having been subjected to severe headaches while praying for brothers and sisters who are bound by the powers which run rampant among us. I can't establish a definite theology here, since the Bible doesn't go into detail, but experience seems to indicate that the enemy is both able and more than willing to lash out at those who would come against him. If that's the case, then all he has to do is refrain from his lashing, my headache goes away, and he says, "See? I have the power to heal!" That's not unlike the cruel little boy who stuffs a kitten in a sack and throws it into the lake. Just before the kitten drowns, he pulls out the sack, releases the poor victim and says, "Aren't you glad I was here to save you?"

Any temptation I feel to listen to those who would call upon forces other than God for healing must be tempered with the realization that those forces are the ones responsible for the disease in the first place. I freely admit my part in the great Fall; I know that by my sin, Eden remains indisputably out of my reach, beyond the flaming sword which would prevent any unlawful return. But I also recognize that the legions under Satan which battle for my very soul are the instruments which would destroy me if they could. Make no mistake: sin is part and parcel of my life: a conscious choice I make to rebel against my Creator and the reason why Jesus Christ had to die on the Cross. But there is another result of sin which is not part of me but is in fact another created entity, an entity that doesn't simply want to kill me, but to humiliate me, to drive me to despair, to destroy my will to resist and cause me to curse the God who made me. By doing so, he not only makes my life miserable, but also makes a statement against the One Who threw him out of Paradise. With his foot on my neck, he grinds his heel all the harder while sneering not at me, but at the God who made me. "Here is what I think of your creation!" he gloats. "I despise him because You love him. I will continue to hurt him because it hurts you." And so the enemy continues his destructive work in the world. And make no mistake: he will not relent until that day when he and all those who follow him are thrown into the Pit forever. Until that time, we can and must resist him. At times, face to face confrontation will be necessary, as we advance to the battle line, take our places alongside the army of God and join the fray. But even more insidious will be the battles we're called upon to wage within our own ranks. Those who would do good in the name of the one whose name is Evil, those who use the spiritual truths of the heavenly realm and twist them into praise for the Destroyer himself: they must be challenged. The ground they stand on must be shown as the quicksand it is. We ourselves must hold the high ground, firmly established on the Rock whose Name is the only one which brings true healing. The magician's lamb is a shrewd adversary. Fear him. Fight him. Flee from him.

For Discussion:

1. Have you ever been involved in spiritual power which you knew did not come from God?

2. What would you say to someone who offered to use that power (above) for the sake of something good?

3. What images do you have of Satan? Where did those images come from?

For further study and background:

Find references in the Bible which refer to spiritualists, mediums and anyone who would try and harness those powers apart from God. From those, what can you deduce concerning our own involvement in such things?

A few examples:

1. Leviticus 20:27
2. Deuteronomy 18:10–11
3. 1 Samuel 28
4. 1 Chronicles 10:13
5. Acts 13

Chapter Seven

The Demon Lamb

You believe there is one God. Good! Even the demons believe that – and shudder.

James (James 2:19)

The top of the mountain is getting closer. Even in the darkness, the sensation of height is a growing feeling. I catch myself thinking about stepping off the trail and falling down the sheer abyss I know is there. All the way to the bottom of the mountain. I wouldn't fall on purpose, of course... but still, to be down there, rather than up here...

It's getting harder to breathe, but I don't think it's because of the altitude, and I know it's not fatigue. Death waits just above us, and a part of me has already begun to die. Anger no longer lives, nor denial. Any hope of finding a scapegoat, a trade, or any magic formula has died during the journey. There's nothing left inside the shell of my body but the remnants of a broken heart kept alive by the short gasping breaths, and by a vague sense of resolve to carry out what was begun. I'm not looking for lambs anymore; there won't be any. All that's left is the act itself: an act so reprehensible I can't bear to think of it, it, much less talk about it with my son. So we both walk on, side by side but each in our own worlds which we share with no man.

The thunder, which has been a constant reminder from above of the journey's end, has stopped. The clouds still cover the peak, and occasional fingers of mist sweep down to surround us in even greater darkness. Now as we walk, the silence is complete, the darkness total. The only sound is that of our breathing, shallow and rapid, but strangely in cadence with one another. I realize that we're walking at the same pace; is he matching my breathing or am I matching his? The sound is somehow comforting, and while it stirs no hope from within my shattered heart, still it offers an unspoken message: a message which if given words might sound like, "It's all right. It's all right. It's all right."

I listen to the message for awhile, as we keep going up through the dark silence. Suddenly I'm aware of a break in the rhythm. Something is out of step. I try to adjust my pace to match my son's, but it doesn't help. It's still there: the discordant sound. A wave of nausea sweeps over me as I begin to understand that the sound is neither from me nor from my son. There's is a third source.

We stop. He must have heard it too. For more than a minute, we hold our breaths, all of our senses tuned to detect the slightest intrusion. There it is, off to the left. A breathing sound, but not regular. As if it's trying to hold its breath too, but not succeeding. I strain to see, but the darkness hides all traces of the Third Source: all but the irregular breathing.

"Who is it?" I tremble at last. "Identify yourself." This time the breathing stops and remains silent for a long time. Then it begins again.

I try to muster a confidence I don't feel, and raise my voice. "I command you in the Name of the One who sent me here, speak up!"

With that, two catlike eyes suddenly become visible. They had evidently been closed before. The Source is less than six feet away, and from the eyes I judge it to be slightly taller than myself.

"You command me to speak? Very well. But you won't like what I have to say."

"I'll be the judge of that," I say, involuntarily stepping back away from the eyes. "Who are you, and what are you doing here?"

"I am the one you warn others against, and I am here to watch a killing."

The eyes close for a moment, and fear sweeps over me like a cold wind. Where is he? Has he moved? I'm just about to run in panic when the eyes open again, and I can see that he's still in the same place as before.

"What do you mean 'warn against'? I don't even know you. How could I warn others against you?"

"Oh you know me all right. I've never been too far away. At times you even invite me a little closer. But most of the time we simply enjoy a mutually contemptible relationship. That is, until you began dabbling in forbidden areas, lashing out at things you know nothing about. You've made my life, and the lives of my friends extremely uncomfortable. But all of that is in the past now. You will bother us no more."

"Why do you say that?" I ask with less

conviction than I feel, all the while testing the ground around my feet for a stone large enough to use as a weapon.

"Don't you know yet why you've been thrust up on this lovely mountain? It's because of me!" he shouts, then, as if thinking better of it, lowers his voice to a hoarse whisper. "*I* am responsible for your being here, and *you* are at fault. You dared to tread upon me, and now you will pay with the life of your son."

"No!" I scream, but my voice can't hide the question.

"Yes," he whispers back. "You are at fault. And when you go back down this mountain *alone,* remember this: I can strike whenever and wherever I please. Back away, or we will meet here again."

—

Somehow Christians have gotten the idea that spiritual warfare is some kind of word game. If the televangelists are to be believed, it's not unlike a video arcade, where the bad guys explode all around us in little flashes of light and a tiny "zap!". Often, it never occurs to us that the bad guys might hit back. On one level that simply adds an element of realism to the game. I know Who holds the final victory, so let the sabers fly. I'll end up at the foot of the throne bloodied but undefeated. But tragically, personal injury isn't the only threat. Satan might also strike those I love. Remember all those adventures, when the hero is bound in the clutches of the arch villain? "You'll never get me to talk!" he declares through clenched teeth. "Do your worst!" But as it turns out the villain's worst is far more despicable than our hero imagined. Suddenly he produces the heroine, who gives a quiet whimper. "Maybe *this* will loosen your tongue," the villain suggests while looking at the heroine. It works every time. The hero crumbles, and eventually has to find another way to bring the bad guys to justice.

I don't know if Hollywood learned the trick from the enemy, or if the enemy learned it from Hollywood, but make no mistake, the threat of injury to a loved one is a powerful deterrent to any child of God. On the surface, it sounds pretty compelling: "Call yourself a Christian, if you must. Do your duty from time to time. You'll enjoy the acclaim of your position and spend eternity in Heaven as you wish. But take one step over the line, and your loved ones will feel my wrath."

This is an issue which no Christian can afford to overlook. There's too much at stake, and the hazards are too great not to confront. Two questions have to be asked, and they must be settled: *Does* Satan have the kind of power he claims to have, and does it make any difference if he does?

To even begin to try and find an answer, we have to go to the only source proven to be trustworthy: the Word of God. Everything else must be understood in light of what we find there; otherwise we become hopelessly bogged down in speculation. In the first place, we need to recognize that Satan does indeed have a certain degree of influence over the world. Sin has paid a deadly toll on God's creation, and for that we have to credit the Evil One. However, let's take a closer look at just *how* he has accomplished his work of destruction. From the very beginning, in the Garden of Eden, everything was good. Man was blessed with every joy imaginable, including the freedom of choice. The tree of the knowledge of good and evil was there for him to look at, and by a conscious decision on his part to choose obedience and deny himself that experience. Satan could have helped himself all he wanted to from the tree, and it wouldn't have made a bit of difference to man. For sin to come into the world, the man would have to choose to disobey. By the same token, it wouldn't have done for Satan to have carried Adam bodily to the tree, forced his mouth open and made him eat from it. That would have only brought Satan the wrath of God, and Adam wouldn't have been any closer to sin than before. So whether Satan *had* the power to force the issue or not is irrelevant. His only effective weapon was deception.

God reminded man of his authority over the Deceiver when He warned Cain about the road he was traveling. "Why is your face downcast? If you do what is right, will you not be accepted? But if you do not do what is right, sin is crouching at your door; it desires to have you, but you must master it" (Gen. 4:6–7).

From this I conclude two things: the enemy is never far away. He's as close as my heart's door, in fact. But his ability to touch me depends upon *my* actions. In spite of the fact that "he wants to have me,"

I can and must learn to master him. Cain heard this, but he didn't listen, and I think it's important to point out here that *Satan* did not kill Able; Cain did it himself, having been deceived into believing it would accomplish something to his advantage.

Deception is the Enemy's most efficient tool, and make no mistake, he uses it well. However you choose to interpret the book of Job, the truth it communicates about Satan is worth remembering: he was never able to lay a finger on Job until he had permission to do so, and even then there were clearly-defined limits to what he could do. "He is in your hands," God decreed, "but you must spare his life" (Job 2:6). From that one example, we have tried to build entire theologies of God's dealings with Satan and Satan's dealings with Man, which I'm rather hesitant to do. But one thing I think we do need to remember from this account as a whole is this: the amount of power which Satan did or did not employ on Job was not his primary method of attack. Rather, it was the deception which followed, as Job's three friends and even his own wife tried to convince him that he was something less in God's sight than he had believed himself to be.

Where does real power lie? The richest men in the world will tell you it's not in money, but in influence. A truckload of cash is worthless to the man who can be convinced to spend it in any way the convincer wishes. Sickness, persecution and adversity are just tools in the Enemy's hand. The real accomplishments he's after are not necessarily to hurt us, although I'm sure he takes great delight in doing so, but in convincing us in the midst of our pain and suffering, as Job's wife insisted, to "curse God and die" (Job 2:9). Even if he could make a man's life from birth to death one unending chain of agony, he knows that would be insignificant in the scope of eternity. Better still, get a man to take his precious gift of eternal life, bought with the blood of Christ and promised to all who will receive it, and throw it on the ground, spit on it and say to the Lord, "I reject You and everything You stand for!" Now *that's* an accomplishment which will have eternal significance.

I came dangerously close to such deceptions in my journey up the mountain of grief. When God failed to act as I thought He should, the Deceiver was right there with plenty of reasons. "He doesn't care about you or your son," I was told. "He's powerless to do anything about it. He likes to watch you suffer." I never bought into those ridiculous statements. But the fact that I listened to them so intently, turning them over and over in my mind, trying them on for size, is an indication of how desperate I was for answers: any answers which would speak to my misery.

God in His wisdom has not granted us all the answers we seek: not yet. Instead, He asks us to trust Him and keep moving forward by faith. Are we any different with our own children? I could explain to my four-year-old the importance of sexual abstinence, or to my eight-year-old the consequences of voting a straight one party ticket, but I think the time might be better spent playing Old Maid or chasing a ball. This is not to say they won't need to know these things eventually, but they must learn them in proportion to their level of maturity. And let's face it, in things of the spirit, we're all still babes in the woods.

I can hear some of you saying now, "But you still haven't answered the question of power... does Satan have it or not?" You're right, and the reason is, I can't answer that question, at least to my own complete satisfaction. There are times when he does seem to have a limited ability to make me sick (such as every time I think about him), and the proliferation of pain and suffering among innocent children seems to tell me that not all the misery in this world is self-inflicted. But in the light of Scripture, I have to balance all this with one over-riding fact: God is the final authority in all things, and not one event escapes His notice nor His control. The words of Jesus to His disciples are a little disquieting, as He alludes to the power the Enemy *does* have, but then I am comforted as the point is made:

"Do not be afraid of those who kill the body but cannot kill the soul. Rather, be afraid of the One who can destroy both soul and body in hell."

(Matt. 10:28)

I accept that, Lord, and I rejoice in the fact that You have power over body and soul; but what was that You said about "killing the body"? I *like* my body. Is there no hope in this world? Jesus goes on:

"Are not two sparrows sold for a penny? Yet not one of them will fall to the ground apart from the will of your Father. And even the very hairs of your head are all numbered. So don't be afraid; you are worth more than many sparrows."

(Matt. 10:29–31)

There's the point: yes, bodies get killed, sparrows fall, and precious children get leukemia. This is part of the fallen world we live in. But this is not to say we are helpless before it. For the glory of God, we *will* see victories over disease and death. Demons *will* be held at bay and the Light of the Gospel *will* shine into every corner of the world. But the real victory is the one Satan wanted most: not the daily miseries he manages to deal out from the short chain he's been tied to, but the eternal victory: the victory over sin and death for all time, and the destruction once and for all of the Deceiver and his followers. That's a victory we can't see yet, from our earthbound perspectives. But be assured Satan sees it quite well, and for all of his deceptive, corrupting work, can't do a thing to change it.

And so I hope this answers the second question we must all address: what difference does it make if Satan *does* have the power to hurt us or our loved ones? Will negotiating with him help our situation in the least? If there's one thing we should all understand by now, it's this: Satan is not a negotiator, he's a deceiver. If you think you can "strike a bargain" with him whereby you and your family can somehow avoid unpleasantries, think again. He's going to do nothing to your advantage, no matter what he seems to promise. The best hope you have in dealing with him is to "put on the full armor of God so that you can stand against the devil's schemes" (Eph. 6:11). Don't negotiate, don't beg, don't ask for mercy from him, and don't give any either. He wants nothing less than your soul, and is never farther away than your door. Don't lose sight of the fact that God is, and always will be in absolute control. You have nothing to fear as long as your mind is fixed on Him.

—

"'Back away,' I said," the voice in the darkness repeats. "Mind your own business, or I assure you, you *will* travel this road again. And who might be your companion next time?"

In spite of the coolness of the air and the flowing mist around us, I feel a flush come to my face and beads of sweat along my forehead. Is this the lamb I've been seeking? Not an innocent animal which I could lay on the altar in place of my son, but a creature of power with whom I can negotiate? The top of the mountain is so near; if there is ever to be a rescue, it has to be here, and now. What if I could overpower him, kill him, and take his wretched body to the top? Would that result in any kind of mercy from *Him*? I think about my chances; he's larger than me, and I suspect that he's somehow able to see in the darkness better than I can. He obviously possesses abilities far beyond mine, since he knows so much about me. But still, he has eyes, a voice, and he *breathes*! He's no more than a creature. And what have I become during this journey, but a creature myself, devoid of all hopes, dreams, love of life? All I want is to see my son live. If I die trying to accomplish that, then I'll die satisfied. Before me stands the embodiment of all that is evil. He was right: I *have* warned others about him. Now I'll rid the world of him, throw his carcass at the feet of God and say, "*Now* release my son from the curse!"

My right foot finds a stone, not much bigger than an orange, but it will have to do. In one motion, I bend down, sweep the stone into my hand and leap toward the eyes, which are now glaring at me. But instead of finding his flesh, I strike what seems like a solid wall of rock and fall back, the weapon flying from my hand. Blood is gushing from my head, and the world seems to be spinning. Those eyes open wider until they look twice as big as before, and that voice rings out in victory, "You see what your pitiful attempts on me are worth. *Human*! You are weak, and I curse you for your weakness. *I* would have smashed your miserable body out of existence long ago, but *He* decided to keep you. The fool! Doesn't He see what a worthless mass of clay you are? Now, *human*, you will see what power *I* have! *This* is what I was cast out of Heaven for, and this is how I deal with those *He* would save!"

I close my eyes, expecting at any moment to feel sharp talons wrenching my heart out. For all my brokenness, in spite of the dead hopes and dreams I've cherished, still there remains within me a spark of desire. I want to live! "God!" I cry out, "Save me!"

My eyes are still closed, but suddenly the world is as bright as day. No covering could shut out the light which pours in from all directions. I open my eyes, and find that the night has turned to day in an instant. Directly overhead, there's an object, brighter than the sun, too dazzling to look at but too awesome to ignore. The trail is still there, and as I look down the mountain, I can see every stop I've made along the way. The lambs which had confronted me are there too, in plain sight, but like me they're cringing from the light. Rising directly in front of me is a cliff, its rock face smooth as glass, except for a tiny ledge about six feet off the ground. And there, perched in terror, is the creature I had feared. He's about the size of a small rabbit, his catlike eyes disproportionately large for his body. He's trembling, looking up at the light, then burying his head in his tiny paws. Looking around, I see the stone I had lost. Grabbing it up, I move toward the thing. "So this is the 'awesome power' of the night," I say sarcastically. *You* are the one who would kill my son? Take a last look around you *creature*, because it's going to be your last."

I raise my hand to strike the miserable object before me, but before I can do so, a wave of paralysis sweeps over me. The stone falls from my hand, and my arm drops uselessly to my side. In a moment of panic, I look back up to the creature on the ledge, but he's still trembling, taking no notice of me whatsoever. From the light above, a voice rings out and buries itself in my very soul. "It is not yours to destroy what I have created. His fate is in my hands, and I will deal with him as I see fit... just as I will with you."

The voice is now silent, but there are no other words necessary. All that's needed to be said has been said. The light, which just a moment before was so impossibly bright, now grows smaller, then moves up to the top of the mountain. The demon may still be where he was before. I don't know, and I don't care anymore. My son may be with me, or he may have gone on ahead. All I know is that the light waits above, and that's where I want to be. With a lightness to my feet I've never felt before, I stand and continue to walk: upward, to the top.

For discussion:

1. Does the existence of an unseen, spiritual world cause you difficulty?

2. Paul says to take a stand against spiritual evil (Ephesians 6:11 ff); are we prepared to do that?

3. Can a person become so focused on defeating Satan that he loses his focus on God?

For further study and background:

Consider Paul's words about spiritual battle in Ephesians 6. Then consider these factors:

1. Mankind is the focus of a battle we can't even see

2. Negotiation is never an option

3. Victory is assured

4. Injury is a possibility

How do these make you feel?

Chapter Eight

The Lamb of Lambs

I wept and I wept because no one was worthy to open the scroll or look inside...
Then I saw a lamb, looking as if it had been slain, standing in the centre of the throne...

John (Rev. 5:4–6)

For eight months, our family suffered through hope and disappointment, courage and despair as our son died of leukemia. I often wonder which would be better: to lose a child suddenly and without warning, such as in a horrific accident, or to have the process stretched out over months? Which would be better: for your child to be too young to understand what's happening and only be able to cry tears of ignorance, or to know full well the specter that surrounds and sucks the life from you one day at a time? As I write this, I know that I'm still in grief. I know, because he is still the first thing on my mind when I wake up every morning. For the most part, I can function now as any responsible husband and father should: I go to work, I pay the bills, I even laugh occasionally. But I know I'm in grief, because at any moment I can lose my grip. Opening a drawer and finding something of his unexpectedly, a song, a word, a thought, anything could tear away the paper walls I've managed to prop around my broken heart, leaving me wounded and crying. Writing this manuscript is almost the hardest thing I've ever done in my life. The hardest thing was the living of it.

But I'm driven by an intense desire to see this through, even before I leave this cabin where I've gone away to be alone in order to write. I know at least part of the reason I'm so compelled to do this, and I suspect you know as well. Grief is a debilitating, gut-wrenching force; but it's also a creative force, firing up something within a person's deepest being, urging expression. And expression is part of the healing process. So, in committing this experience to words, I'm helping myself to heal. That's the selfish motivation. But there is another, and I hope deeper incentive to this effort. Throughout this ordeal, people in grief have ministered to me in ways that no one else could ever have done. C. S. Lewis in *A Grief Observed* asked a lot of the questions I was asking, and although he, like myself, was unable to find many satisfying answers, knowing that his hurt was similar to my own somehow made mine easier to bear. I didn't want to read John Claypool's *Tracks of a Fellow Struggler* while Trevor was alive; his situation was too close to mine, and I knew that his daughter had died of leukemia. Reading it, I felt, would be too much like accepting defeat before the battle was over. In the first week after losing Trevor, though, I read of Rev. Claypool's journey and was profoundly blessed. Catherine Marshall's collection of journal entries related to the death of her granddaughter in *Light in My Darkest Night* filled out the rest of my hollow places, as she had to deal with the problem of a healing God who refused to heal. I know that I am far from being completely recovered, but I know also that I have progressed much farther than I would have were it not for these grief-stricken people who allowed themselves to be used by God during that critical time.

So I must write this now, while the memory is still fresh, and the wounds are still open and visible. I know that in time, by God's grace, my agony will be diminished and the memories which cause so much hurt today will be mercifully forgotten or filed in the far reaches of my mind. For that reason, I need to express this now so that it will minister to another's grief.

John Claypool wrote of the "Brotherhood of the Hurting," and I count myself as a member. Knowing that it's not by any great achievement that one gains entry, but rather through shared loss, I include my name alongside Claypool, Lewis and Marshall as individuals who have made the journey all the way to the top of the mountain, and have seen the Lamb of Lambs there.

Looking back along the way, we can all recognize the great pretenders who lie in wait for every pilgrim making the ascent against his will. Anger, Denial, Warrior, Trade, Scapegoat, Magician and Demon are all there, and will take every opportunity at their disposal to try and dissuade a person's faith in God at a time when that faith is more vital than ever. And there are other lambs on the mountain as well. Fellow travelers have reported meeting creatures that sound like nothing I have ever encountered, nor would I want to. But I think that the fact I did not meet them merely says that their temptations would not have been as effective with me. We each have our weaknesses, and the Enemy knows those well. We may be assured that the attacks we must endure have been especially designed with us in mind. For some, the temptation to "curse God and die" as our brother Job heard would elicit no meaningful response, while the Lamb of Trade might have just the thing which would cause another grieving climber to stop and consider. The end result is that those lambs we encounter do look formidable indeed, as in fact they are. But we of the Brotherhood want to say to you that the lambs we meet have nothing to compare with the Lamb who waits at the top. I know that may be difficult to believe, especially when it would seem that we have lost the cause. Our nightmares became reality. We cannot testify to miraculous healing. For us there are no rams caught in the thicket, but only what was promised from the beginning: grief and loss, followed by more grief.

But I say again, there is a Lamb up here, and He's like no other lamb you may meet along the way. The others offer temporary relief from the moment, and even those are false promises. But this Lamb gives meaning to the moment, and turns the moment into an eternity of joy and hope and peace.

When I was ten years old, I prayed that I wouldn't have to have my tonsils out. They were inflamed, and the common first treatment in those days was prompt removal. The thought terrified me. I'd been a Christian for about a year by then, and was beginning to learn that Jesus was concerned with my daily struggles. This was the biggest struggle I'd been faced with to date, and I prayed with every ounce of feeling I could muster. "*Please* don't let them take my tonsils out," I pleaded. They didn't, and I was one happy boy. My tonsils have never bothered me since then, and I give God the glory for that. But you know, if that prayer had been refused, and I had gone on to surgery, what would have happened? I would have had a couple of days of discomfort, a lot of ice cream and some great stories to tell. And today, as an adult starting to think about retirement, my throat would feel just about the same as it does now, tonsils intact. What I'm trying to say is, the agony we feel at any particular moment is diminished by time. Losing a son is a lot more agonizing than losing tonsils, and I don't believe that even years from now I'll be able to look back on this time in the same way that I look back on that day as a child in the doctor's office. But there is another perspective from which I have yet to experience, and that is from outside this time of physical life. From God's point of view, our daily struggles can't possibly compare to the eternity He's prepared for us. As the familiar hymn says, "When we've been there ten thousand years, bright shining as the sun, we've no less days to sing God's praise than when we first begun." That verse of Amazing Grace, by John Newton, has always bothered me, I have to confess. For myself, a "long time" is counted in hours, not years; or even minutes, if I'm sitting in the dentist's chair. The idea of "being" in Heaven for ten thousand years, and then coming to the realization that my time remaining is no less than it was from the first day I arrived may sound great when I sing it, but from my time-bound life on this earth, it is simply incomprehensible. Obviously, there is something about "time" and my understanding of it that is lacking when I try to imagine what Heaven will be like.

Looking at it that way, the pain and suffering we endure now is really only a passing thing, and something which will make sense "in time". It seems that it would be easy for God to say, "It won't last forever. Get over it." But that's not our kind of God. Our God knows what a trivial thing our grief is in the scope of eternity, but that doesn't keep Him from stepping into our lives, in our times of grief, and ministering to us. He doesn't belittle us for our ignorance in the face of eternity, but gently holds us in His powerful arms and whispers words of comfort, much like a loving mother or father would do for a precious child who is hurting.

I suppose God could have arranged some method whereby the Lamb would have simply been sacrificed for our sins and gone back to the Father's side. Perhaps it could have even taken place outside the scope of time, so that we wouldn't even be aware of it. But that's not the way it happened. The Son of God stepped into time and space to share our suffering and endure our grief, twenty-four hours a day, just like us. He had to agonize over His coming crucifixion, desperately seeking another way. The Father could have told Him, "In the bigger scope of things, You won't even notice this. Get over it."

But He didn't. In fact, God didn't even tell His Son that it was going to be all right. Instead, He turned His back on Him, and let Jesus experience the depths of despair. Was all that really necessary? Certainly not for Jesus' sake, but perhaps instead for mine. With that thought, I don't feel quite so alone on the mountain top. My son has gone on to be with God, but the Lamb is still here, and He's saying to me, "I know how you feel. I've been there."

I can't say the same thing to you, fellow climber. I don't know exactly how you feel. The road of grief is an intensely personal thing, and cannot be shared with another, not completely. But the Lamb is intensely personal, too. He has that unique ability to come into your heart, experience your grief, and then heal it. The healing will probably not be instantaneous, and I'm sure there's a good reason for that. I suspect it's related to the fact that life itself is not instantaneous, but an experience to be lived. Unlike the heavens and the earth, which came to be as a result of a spoken Word, there was a process involved in the creation of humanity which makes us unique from everything else. We were lovingly crafted from the dust of the ground, and the breath of life was breathed into our nostrils from the Creator Himself. It took time, and it took a personal kind of love such as only God could give.

The healing experience is a kind of growth, and

growth also takes time. Soon enough, we will leave this prison of time and be set loose into a whole new realm of existence. I pray for that day to come swiftly. But until then, I will experience what God has set before me, and by His grace will try and learn from it, so that when I'm finally able to step off the mountain and be carried to a higher plain, I'll be able to hear, "Well done, good and faithful servant. You've been faithful in a few things; I will put you in charge if many things. Come and share your Master's happiness!"

—

The journey up the mountain has been emotionally and physically exhausting. In desperation, I've searched the path for a lamb which would serve as a substitute for my son on the altar of sacrifice. Anger and Denial were my constant companions, but pitiful comfort. The lamb of Trade couldn't begin to pay the price my son's life demanded, nor could Scapegoat take his place. The Magician's lamb and his brother Demon have taken their toll on my emotions until I stand at the top of the mountain, broken and dejected. My legs give way and I collapse to my knees, hands clasped together in an effort to keep from sprawling face down in the dirt. The light which had so blinded me while at the same time revealed to me the whole path below, had led me on to this summit, but now has disappeared. I'm wondering if I ever really saw it at all. In its place, I'm left in a world of shadows and images which any other time would cause me to fear for my safety. But I'm beyond fear now. Death, even violent and painful death, would be welcomed as a dear friend.

From my knees, I lift my head and see that my son's body lies on a stone altar, just a few paces farther ahead. When did that happen? Now I'm left with the question for which no answer seems possible: How can I ever get back down from this place alone?

A fresh breeze brushes my face, drying the tears and sweat. The blinding mist which has been my constant companion during the entire journey is blown away, and as the clouds lift, the sky seems to grow a little brighter. The altar where my son lies had been shrouded in darkness, but now it's coming into clearer view. Its rough hewn edges seem to threaten any who might try to come near. I want to step forward: to take my son in my arms, to hold him like I had never held him in life, to whisper in his ears the words I never spoke when I had the chance. But the cold, gray stone warns me away, and I remain where I am, on my knees and struggling to hold onto consciousness.

As the clouds lift, I look beyond the stone and see another stone behind it, slightly higher than the one in front. This demands my attention, and I look closer to see another one beyond that. Finally, I realize that what I thought was an altar is in fact only the first of a series of steps leading higher still. Peering through the mist, which is growing lighter by the minute, I can make out the real altar beyond the top most step. It's already occupied.

The Lamb of Lambs is there. I can see at once that He's different from the others I'd encountered on the trail below. I'm amazed that I could have been so easily deceived by them. They're not anything like Him at all. He's so beautiful, so powerful, so... so Perfect. I'm on my knees, and have no intention of moving. Instead, I raise my hands in total surrender, not understanding what that means, but not caring either. I have no care in the world, except for Him: no desire, except to know that I belong to Him. I start to speak, but the words catch in my throat when I realize He's bleeding. A fountain of blood is pouring from a wound in His throat. As I watch in horror, it begins to spill over the altar and run down the sides, finding its way over the steps. I'm frozen in place, unable and at the same time unwilling to move. The blood flows down slowly, one step at a time, until finally it reaches the place where my son lies. First it pools around him, tiny rivulets converging and outlining his cold form, setting him apart from the stone surrounding him. Then the blood begins to cover him, until he's completely enveloped. By now I'm so far removed from the reality of what's happening that any ideas of intervening would be unthinkable. Instead, I'm left with a profound sense of gratitude that I'm allowed the chance to observe this miracle at work.

It comes as no surprise when my son opens his eyes. He doesn't look in my direction, but stands, facing the altar. He waits for only a moment, then begins climbing the steps. At first, his steps are hesitant and unsure, as if the disease which has taken his life still maintains a grip on his limbs. With each step, however, strength returns, and I watch a process which my father's eyes have seen in him before. I watch his uncertain first move, then the hesitant toddler climbing to the next level. And finally I see the young man in his prime, a spring in his step and a strength born of youth, as he fairly bounds over the hurdles. Near the top, he pauses and looks back in my direction. The face is his, all right; there's no doubt about that. But it's not the face of a child anymore. It's a man I'm looking at: a grown, handsome man with the stunning expression of one who has become what he was created to be. His eyes meet mine for a moment, and I see there a depth of love that I've never known in this life: a love devoid of all pretense, all selfish motives, all fear.

There's a twinkle in his eyes that I've seen before on a few occasions. I remember once when he and his mother had gone shopping and brought my birthday present home, wrapped up in beautiful blue paper. "Open it, Dad!" he'd cried, knowing what I was about to know, and beside himself with joy at the prospect of my seeing it for the first time. Watching him standing there, tall and strong, I have to speak: to tell him of my joy for him and how proud he's made me. But before I can open my mouth, he turns back toward the altar and continues on.

My eyes travel upward to the waiting Lamb. He looks down at me and speaks. "Do not be dismayed. Your son is with me, and in the Father's time you will also come up these steps. I am the Lamb you sought. I am the way to life."

The clouds begin blowing up from down below. All too soon, the Lamb, my son, the altar and the steps themselves are hidden from view. I want to climb on, to be where they are; but I know that's not possible. As I turn to start back down the mountain, I'm aware of a tremendous pain in my heart. Was it there all along, or am I just now able to feel it? There's a sense of terrible loss, and a loneliness that scares me. But as I begin to walk, another sense moves in and takes up residence in my heart. There's another Presence inside me, lighting up the darkness and easing the burden. The lambs which had seemed so promising during the journey up the mountain now cower in fear as we pass by. I can see them now for what they are, and I won't be intimidated by them again. From the aching remnants of my heart, a song begins to rise. My steps stretch out for the long journey home, and I begin to sing:

> *The road leads up,*
> *but his thoughts reach out,*
> *What father would not be given to doubt?*
> *The life of his son, in place of a lamb,*
> * To obey without question,*
> *what kind of a man?*
>
> *Looking for a Lamb around every bend,*
> *At the top of the mountain,*
> *dark clouds descend.*
> *A sacrifice waits: a father, a son*
> *To bring to fruition what faith has begun.*

Near the top of the mountain
my son cries in pain,
Will God stay the knife? Will I rise up again?
"Of course," I reply, although we both know
The lamb that we seek is His to withhold

From the top of the mountain,
from a tree higher still,
The Son cries out, a purpose fulfilled.
The Lamb that we sought
is now clearly seen
In the lives of His sons,
from death now redeemed

Looking for a lamb around every bend
At the top of the mountain
dark clouds descend
But through the dim shadow,
by the power of grace
The Lamb we sought after,
now stands face to face.

Printed in the United States
29472LVS00001BA/13-36